EDWIN ARLINGTON ROBINSON

EDWIN ARLINGTON ROBINSON

Edwin Arlington Robinson

BY {YVOR WINTERS}

Janet Lewis, 1899–

THE MAKERS OF MODERN LITERATURE

New Directions Books · Norfolk, Connecticut

811
R659
L

9919

9919

CONTENTS

1. ROBINSON'S LIFE [1]

ROBINSON'S FAMILY ON BOTH SIDES CAME OF OLD NEW ENG-land stock. His father, Edward Robinson, a storekeeper and miscellaneous businessman at Head-of-the-Tide, Maine, came of a family who had long been expert carpenters and shipwrights. His mother, who was born Mary Elizabeth Palmer, was descended from Thomas Dudley, the second colonial governor of Massachusetts, and from Dudley's daughter, Mercy Woodbridge, sister to Ann Bradstreet, the first American poet. The children of this marriage, in the order of birth, were Horace Dean, who was known as Dean, Herman and Edwin Arlington. Shortly after the birth of Edwin, in 1869, the family moved to Gardiner, Maine, a larger town, the Tilbury Town of Robinson's poems.

It was in Gardiner that Robinson grew up. He showed no practical talents, and apparently showed little talent

[1] The facts in this summary are taken from *Edwin Arlington Robinson, A Biography*, by Herman Hagedorn, Macmillan, 1938. This is the only biography of Robinson thus far published.

1

for conventional study, but he read widely and began writing verse while in high school. It was while he was in high school that he met Dr. Alanson Tucker Schumann, a physician and literary amateur, who seems to have been impressed at once with Robinson's ability, and who introduced Robinson to the local literary group. In the light of the fact that Schumann and Robinson were closely associated for a few years and read and criticized each other's poems, it is interesting to note the one poem by Schumann which Hagedorn quotes.

> See the sonnet, "Guidance," page 34, in *Edwin Arlington Robinson, A Biography,* by Herman Hagedorn.

This is not immortal poetry, but in spite of a few trite phrases it has a kind of plain honesty which is not unlike the plain honesty of much of the best of Robinson. Schumann must have been a man of some intelligence, and it is possible that he may have had an influence on the formation of Robinson's style. Hagedorn tells us furthermore [2] that Schumann was devoted to the early French forms, the rondeau, the ballade and the villanelle, and some of Robinson's early work is in these forms.

During these years, Robinson's brother Dean returned home, a drug addict and a drunkard, having taken to narcotics and to alcohol in order to sustain himself through the hardships of his country medical practice. The father was now an old man and failing in health, and Herman was

[2] Hagedorn, op. cit., p. 34.

taking over the family business. Robinson appears to have been considered necessary at home to help look after his father and brother; and his father, feeling that Dean's case proved the worthlessness of a college education, refused to send his son to college. Robinson spent an extra year at high school, and seems to have felt his isolation acutely, with his own class gone; but finally an injury to an ear, the result of a blow given him by a teacher years before, required that he spend a year within reach of a Boston physician; and Herman persuaded their father that he should at the same time be permitted to attend Harvard. Hagedorn tells us that during these years he read Swinburne, Rossetti, Austin Dobson and Thomas Hardy, among others. The last two may have exerted some influence upon him, though in different ways and degrees.

At Harvard, where he registered as a special student, he tried Anglo-Saxon for three weeks with the distinguished Professor Francis Child, but he found the subject too much for him. Among the other members of the Harvard faculty at the time, who were within the range of Robinson's interest, were Charles Eliot Norton, Lewis Gates, Josiah Royce, LeBaron Briggs and Barrett Wendell. Hagedorn tells us that Gates was his favorite teacher during the first year; what significance this fact may have I do not know, for Gates, whose style and thought alike represent a weak imitation of Pater, appears somewhat remote from Robinson, though he may have been more effective in the classroom than on the printed page. Mr. Lloyd Morris, in his book on Robinson,[3] makes much of the transcendentalist

[3] *The Poetry of Edwin Arlington Robinson,* by Lloyd Morris, New York, 1923.

influence of Royce upon Robinson's thought, and Miss Estelle Kaplan [4] is inclined to agree with him; but as I shall eventually try to indicate, Robinson's transcendentalism appears to me fragmentary, occasional, and contrary to the main direction of his thought and achievement; furthermore, it is of so simple a nature that the influence of a professional philosopher such as Royce is hardly necessary to account for it. Among the students at Harvard at this time were William Vaughan Moody, Robert Morss Lovett, William Lyon Phelps, and Hutchins and Norman Hapgood. His favorite writers during these years seem to have included Carlyle, Crabbe, Arnold, Kipling and Emerson. Emerson strikes me as a more natural source than Royce of such transcendentalism as there may be in Robinson; in fact what one might call the folk atmosphere of the upper levels of New England society would suffice. As I shall point out later, there is a somewhat Carlylean quality in Robinson's somewhat vague social thinking. There is a trace of Kipling influence or of Kiplingesque manner running through a few of the shorter poems over a good many years. Arnold, although I see no trace of his influence, would naturally have appealed to a poet of Robinson's intellectual quality. And from Crabbe he may have learned a good deal about the power attainable through simple accuracy.

Before the end of the college year, Robinson was forced to return home, for his father was dying; the death occurred in July. Of the father's last weeks, Hagedorn writes: "His interest in spiritualism had deepened and, in the slow

[4] *Philosophy in the Poetry of Edwin Arlington Robinson,* by Estelle Kaplan. Columbia University Press, 1940.

disintegration of his organism, detached and eerie energies seemed to be released. There were table rappings and once the table came off the floor, 'cutting my universe,' as Robinson told a friend later, 'clean in half.' As the end approached, other articles of furniture began to levitate. Rows of books on a shelf were swept to the floor. It seemed to Robinson that the piano itself were moving. Of these last months with his father, he told a friend 'They were a living hell.' " Of these facts the reader is free to make what he can; but we may safely say that if Robinson's life, like his poems, was for the most part outwardly quiet, it could not have been without inner intensity.

He returned to Harvard for another year, and then left. He had never intended to take a degree, and the family business was now declining. His own share of the family estate had been mostly lost as a result of Herman's investments; Herman had lost money of his own and was beginning to drink; Dean's condition remained about the same. Robinson suffered acute pain from his ear, and he lived in the fear that the damage might reach his brain and cause insanity. He seems to have gone a good way in these years in the development of his later familiar obsession, the obsession with failure in general and with his own limitations in particular. He had a few intimates at this time who must have possessed some intelligence, but his existence appears to have been a very lonely one.

Although he was writing the poems which were to appear in *The Children of the Night*, including such masterpieces as "Luke Havergal" and "The Clerks," he was able to make no impression upon the nation's editors. Hagedorn finds the plainness of his style revolutionary, and finds in this fact the explanation; but I confess that I can find his style little more revolutionary than that of any first-rate writer in any period. It is no plainer than the style of Mrs. Wharton and is little plainer than that of Emerson; but it is accurate with the conscientiousness of genius, and such accuracy is invariably a major obstacle to success. Nothing baffles the average critic so completely as honesty—he is prepared for everything but that; and I have the impression that this has been true in every period.

Late in 1896 Robinson published his first collection of poems privately and at his own expense, through the Riverside Press, under the title: *The Torrent and the Night Before*. Before it came out, his mother died suddenly of black diphtheria; the physician was afraid to attend her, and Dean pulled himself together to serve as physician; the undertaker refused to touch the body, and the three sons laid it in the coffin and drove it to the cemetery in an express wagon, the minister having read the services through the front window from the safety of the porch. A little later, the book of poems, with a few additions and omissions, was republished by Richard J. Badger, at the expense of William Butler, one of Robinson's friends.

In 1897 Robinson left Gardiner for New York, where his life continued in much the same fashion except for a new background and a new circle of acquaintances. As one looks back over the life of this great and austere poet, one may be inclined to feel amusement at some of the company he kept, but in all likelihood the amusement would be unjust both to him and to his friends. He was surrounded by a group of incomplete geniuses, the debris of the intellectual life which one can meet in any large city in any period; such people are failures and are likely to be weak and somewhat foolish, but they sometimes have the perception and intelligence to recognize and to entertain a distinguished man, and in a world of successful mediocrity such ability deserves respect. Robinson already had acquired such friends as Dr. Schumann and William Henry Thorne; he now met Titus Munson Coan, who as a young man had interviewed the elderly Melville with disappointment and bewilderment, and Alfred Louis, of whom Hagedorn writes: "He was a little man in his late sixties, a Jew, bearded like a prophet, with little feet and delicate hands, and a goatish smell as though he slept in a stable. His long frock-coat was green with age and dirt, his waist-coat stained with grease, his collar grimy; his trousers were frayed and his shoes broken; but his eyes had in them the suffering of five thousand years; and when he rose out of a chair to greet a stranger, it seemed, as an English writer said subsequently, 'as though some great figure of history rose to address not me, but the nations of the world.'" Louis is said to have been the original Captain Craig, and to judge from this description of him he might also have been in part the original of "The Wandering Jew." He had had, or claimed to have had, something of a literary and political career in London; he claimed, for example, that he had been portrayed as Mordecai in *Daniel Deronda*. At about the same time Robinson picked up Joseph Lewis French, perhaps the original of Count Pretzel von Würzburger the Obscene, a minor character in "Captain Craig"; of French, Hagedorn says that "he was pudgy, with heavy jowls, looking somewhat like a punctured John Bull on the verge of tears." French haunted Robinson for the rest

7

of his life, borrowing small sums, borrowing or stealing clothes, admiring him, abusing him, endeavoring to get him the Nobel prize, threatening his life, and borrowing five dollars when Robinson was on his deathbed. Robinson's friends were not, of course, entirely of this interesting class; there were among them a number of normal and intelligent people, who liked, admired and helped him, and there were a few, like Josephine Preston Peabody, Edmund Clarence Stedman, Ridgely Torrance and William Vaughan Moody, who had achieved a little literary distinction.

In 1898, as a result of the intervention of Hays Gardiner, Robinson obtained a position at Harvard as a kind of office boy. Robinson apparently would not consider the idea of teaching; Gardiner had recommended him as a confidential clerk or secretary. Nothing much came of it, and this is the only professional connection on record between America's greatest university and America's greatest poet then living; the incident is disheartening but deserves recording. Robinson also made occasional and ineffective efforts at journalism for a few years, but was frustrated by an inherent necessity to say something and say it well.

In the fall of 1899, Dean Robinson died. A little later Robinson returned to New York, to live in hall bedrooms and work on his poetry. *Captain Craig* was refused by most of the leading publishers, and Robinson continued to produce unpublishable poetry. Finally his work reached Houghton Mifflin, recommended by Lewis Gates, George Lyman Kittredge, William Vaughan Moody and others. Bliss Perry, the literary adviser of the firm, and later one of Robinson's friends, seems to have seen little in it, but finally agreed to publish it if any of Robinson's admiring friends would guarantee the costs; and thus the matter was arranged, with Hays Gardiner and Mrs. Laura Richards as the guarantors. The book received some praise, but no more than many others; the magazines continued to refuse his work; he seems to have lived mainly on gifts and loans for a few years, to have sunk into depression, and to have drunk more whisky than was good for him. Finally he received a job as time-checker in the subway, and although he earned his living in this fashion, the work left him exhausted.

In 1905 Theodore Roosevelt became interested in Robinson's work, which had been called to his attention by his son, Kermit, then a pupil at Groton. Roosevelt, after trying to persuade Robinson to accept several positions, succeeded in getting him into a place as special agent of the Treasury, at $2000 per year. Roosevelt invited Robinson to the White House and talked with him at length; he later wrote an article in praise of Robinson's poems, for the *Outlook* and persuaded Scribner's to reissue *The Children of the Night*. For his temerity in writing a critical article, the president was generally abused by the literary experts of the period, and Robinson's poetry was belittled by them; but Roosevelt must have accomplished more toward assisting Robinson at this juncture with regard both to his reputation and to his personal life than anyone else had done. It is curious to note that Roosevelt found "Luke Havergal" and "Two Gardens in Linndale" obscure, although fortunately for Robinson he shared with the critics of a later generation a liking for poetry which he could not understand.

9

Among the new friends whom Robinson was now acquiring were Percy MacKaye, Louis Ledoux, one of those who gave Robinson a good deal of financial help, May Sinclair, who wrote with admiration of his poetry, and Isadora Duncan, who endeavored unsuccessfully to seduce him. The interest of Robinson's friends in the theater affected Robinson himself for a time, and he wrote *Van Zorn* and *The Porcupine*, which were published several years later. MacKaye, Torrence and Moody were working at plays, and Robinson's poem "The White Lights" was written to celebrate the success of *The Great Divide*, a play by Moody. Robinson's plays were not produced, but his interest in the form may have left a mark, not wholly a good one, on his long poems, which were to be composed later, since these are written largely in scenes which proceed for the most part through conversations. His brother Herman, long since a failure in business and something of an alcoholic, died of tuberculosis in 1908 in a public ward of the Boston City Hospital. Robinson had long been sending what money he could to Herman's family, and his dramatic ambition was in a good measure motivated by a desire to send more. In 1909 Taft succeeded Roosevelt to the presidency, and the new administration in the Customs House demanded that Robinson keep regular hours and do the regular work; Roosevelt had given Robinson the position as a sinecure, explicitly and simply, and Robinson had no knowledge of what the work was supposed to be; so he now resigned.

In 1911 Robinson was persuaded against his judgment to spend the summer at the MacDowell colony, at Peterborough, New Hampshire, and he was so pleased with his life there that he went regularly each summer for the rest of his life. The MacDowell farmhouse, Hillcrest, provided the title and something of the subject for one of his greatest short poems. During this first summer, and for some time thereafter, he worked at fiction and drama, in the hope of making money, but he seems to have lived chiefly by gifts from his friends. He gave up alcohol at this time, in the hope of accomplishing more work; it was a difficult thing to do, for he had been dangerously addicted to drink for at least seven years, and the weakness was one which ran in his family. His poem "The Valley of the Shadow" was the result of his meditation on these years of alcoholism and discouragement. He finally abandoned the idea of succeeding in fiction or in drama, and began writing verse again in some quantity. In 1916 he published *The Man Against the Sky*. Since *The Town Down the River* in 1910 his reputation had grown a little, and a few of the newer poems had been published in magazines. The new book received a good deal of praise, though less than it deserved, and his reputation was now respectable and secure, if not brilliant. The free verse movement had grown during these years, and the great reputations were those of the sentimentalists of the new movement, as the great reputations of his youth had been those of the genteel popularizers of theoretical abandon. "Eros Turannos," one of the greatest short poems in the language, appeared in the same issue of *Poetry* with Carl Sandburg's first group of *Chicago Poems*, which included the poem entitled "Chicago"; Sandburg's group was given the position of honor and at the end of the year received the award of the Levinson Prize, the most considerable prize offered for poetry in the United

States at that time. Robinson's reputation still had no great monetary value; but Hays Gardiner had left him a legacy of $2000, and about the time that this sum was exhausted, Lewis Isaacs got eleven others to join him in providing Robinson $1200 a year, a sum which came to him through the New York Trust Company.

In 1919 the New York *Times Review of Books,* instigated by MacKaye, published an issue celebrating Robinson's fiftieth birthday. There were tributes of one sort or another from Bliss Perry, Vachel Lindsay, Anna Hempstead Branch, Amy Lowell, Edwin Markham and a number of others. In October, 1921, Macmillan published the first collected edition of Robinson's poems, which received the Pulitzer prize for poetry, other special honors and general praise; Robinson was established as a great living classic, but he was still far from achieving the popularity which might have rendered him independent. During the years that immediately followed he was writing some of his greatest short poems and poems of medium length, but was devoting much of his energy to the earlier of the mediocre long poems which were to occupy progressively more and more of his energy. The Prohibition Amendment moved him to return to alcohol, apparently out of indignation, but he was not again dangerously addicted to it. He managed a visit of a few weeks to England, a country to which his fame had not preceded him but where he met a few old friends such as May Sinclair and Alfred Noyes.

In 1927 the publication of *Tristram,* a poem distinctly inferior to *Merlin* and to *Lancelot,* which had appeared before it, was enormously successful, and for the first time his poetry began to bring him an income of tangible value;

he was able now to do without further assistance from Lewis Isaacs and his eleven co-guarantors, and he could even afford a number of minor luxuries and give a diagnostic laboratory to the Gardiner hospital in memory of his brother Dean. In January of 1935 he was forced to enter the New York Hospital, where an exploratory operation revealed a cancer which could not be removed without the shortening of his life; he died there the following March, after having corrected the proofs of his last poem, *King Jasper*.

2. THE NEW ENGLAND BACKGROUND

THE EARLY ENGLISH SETTLERS IN NEW ENGLAND WERE A CARE-
fully selected group. Their religious tenets, Calvinism in theology and Congregationalism in Church government, were disliked by authority in England to the extent that it was unsafe to profess them; whatever the defects of these tenets, the men who held them in the face of danger were men of moral integrity and intensity; those who risked the desperate venture in New England were even more obviously so. It is not surprising, therefore, to find a certain consistency of character in the New Englanders or to find certain New England strains which produce men of unusual ability with remarkable frequency. The Adamses and Holmeses and Lowells are well-known examples of such families, but if one studies pedigrees one is impressed with many examples likewise of descent through the female line, where the relationships are obscured by changes of name. Ann Bradstreet, for example, may be called the mother of American poetry in more senses than one; and

14

Robinson, we have seen, though not descended from her, was descended from her sister. The original settlers, then, were people who were drawn toward certain religious ideas and who had sufficient moral energy to risk life and wealth for their convictions; they must have had certain characteristics in common, and the characteristics must have been strong ones. But once the settlers were established in New England, these characteristics were strongly reinforced by the ideas themselves and by the isolation in which the ideas and the process of breeding to a type were then able to function.

The most important Calvinistic doctrines were the doctrine of man's utter depravity (as distinct from the Catholic doctrine of man's corruption), the doctrine of God's Decrees and the doctrine of predestination. According to the first, man was wholly lost in sin and abominable in the sight of God; according to the second, God had ordained from eternity every detail, no matter how trivial, in the history of the universe; according to the third, God had selected, out of his infinite goodness, a few souls for salvation, the selection having been arbitrary and irrespective of any virtues which those or other souls might appear to have. The last doctrine is merely a subsidiary heading of the second, for if all events are decreed, then the fate of each soul is decreed; and it is closely related to the first, for if man is wholly depraved, he is incapable of true virtue, and if God chooses to save him it is for inscrutable reasons. These concepts, and others related, tended to encourage a highly allegorical frame of mind in the public at large; it became customary to read all events for their significance as part of the divine plan. They tended also to reinforce the moral nature of the Puritan indirectly; logically, these doctrines should have relieved the Puritan of moral responsibility, but actually there was an assumption that election would show itself in conduct, so that the Puritan studied his own behavior assiduously to discover the signs of his election, and it was only human that he should study his neighbor's behavior even more assiduously than his own. Life was incredibly hard, moreover, in early New England, and only the energetically moral could hope to survive.

There was a central contradiction in the Calvinistic doctrine, however, which over a century and a half led to the gradual abandonment of the doctrine: man's acts were decreed, yet man was damned for his sins. The New Englander's moral sense in the long run proved stronger than his loyalty to Calvin, and little by little the doctrine of predestination disappeared; what was ultimately left, at any rate in the more intellectual society, was Unitarianism, a religion which emphasized morality and minimized theological dogmas. Robinson appears to have come from Unitarian stock, to have inherited the traditional moral sense and moral curiosity, which are the sources of his better poems, and to have broken easily with the few remnants of theology which Unitarianism retained. Like a good Unitarian, however, he seems to have remained unconvinced of the need for the precise definition of general ideas.

But the early Calvinism of Europe contained another element, originally the most important of all. It taught that one might be reasonably sure of one's election by virtue of inner assurance, a more or less mystical communion with

God, frequently very violent in its emotional form. The first generation of Calvinists in New England found this doctrine dangerous to society, and substituted for it the concept that one might believe oneself of the elect if one entered the church and conformed to its principles, a belief which strengthened the allegorizing habit, for it made every act symbolic of a man's spiritual state. But the mystical element in Calvinism was not suppressed by this modification; it merely remained more or less beneath the surface; and it was revived in the eighteenth century by Jonathan Edwards, who taught a highly evangelical and emotional kind of religion, whatever the learning and ingenuity with which he expounded it.

The mystical tendency in New England was very strong, and Unitarianism gave it no nourishment; in the nineteenth century, when Calvinism was dead so far as the man of intellect was concerned, Emerson gave a new form and a new impetus to the tendency. Emerson took the essential doctrines of European romanticism and restated them in the language of Edwardian Calvinism. He taught that God and the Universe, mind and matter, are one; that emotion and instinct are not only the true guides to virtue but the voice of God, the operation of Grace; that surrender to this guidance is equivalent to the experience of the mystic. In fact, he went farther than this, for he taught that through surrender to this guidance one not only communes with God but becomes God. Emerson himself was a product of New England and a man of strong moral habits. He seems to have mistaken habit, or second nature, for nature; since his habits were good, he believed that his na-

17

ture was good. He gave to American romanticism, in spite of its irresponsible doctrine, a religious tone which it has not yet lost and which has often proved disastrous. He gave also a kind of moral and religious sanction to mere eccentricity, to self-satisfaction and to critical laziness. The type of mind which follows its first guesses in matters of opinion and perception, with irritated contempt for opposing arguments, and which finds any kind of careful thinking beneath the dignity of a gentleman, is his legitimate heir and can find explicit justification in his writings. This kind of mind is common in modern New England (and no doubt elsewhere); and commingled with the New England moral sense and moral curiosity, there is a good deal of this intellectual laziness in Robinson; and as a result of the laziness, there is a certain admixture of Emersonian doctrine, which runs counter to the principles governing most of his work and the best of it. This tendency does not result in stylistic eccentricity in Robinson, as it does, for example, in much of Emerson and Frost; but it results in loose thinking and in a good many failures of structure. It is the moralistic tradition which predominates in Robinson, however: in the choice of matter, this shows itself in the moral curiosity with regard to the particular case; in the realm of style, in honesty of statement and clarity of form; in the conduct of life, in immutable adherence to a purpose. It is true that Robinson's life shows a good deal of what seems weakness when it is examined with reference to ordinary and practical standards; but it is likewise true that Robinson showed extreme tenacity of purpose in achieving a notable end, and that we are all of us incalculably his debtors. Many of Robinson's best poems, more-

18

over, deal with characters very much like himself, characters who are weak or insignificant in the eyes of the world, but who sustain themselves in loneliness on some kind of inner integrity.

3. LITERARY INFLUENCES ON ROBINSON'S STYLE

THE INFLUENCE OF NEW ENGLAND UPON ROBINSON IS THE influence of a place and a culture upon his mind and character; one can find the same influence at work upon other major writers of New England, but it would be difficult, I believe, to show the influence of any single New England writer upon Robinson, except in so far as Emerson may directly or indirectly have influenced in some small measure his thinking. I shall point out later that the structural method of many of Robinson's long poems has a good deal in common with the method of Henry James; this may be due to the influence of James upon Robinson, directly or through others; or it may be the result of a common background; the similarity is one of general method, in any event, rather than of style. The individual poets who seem to have influenced Robinson's actual style are all British.

Robinson wrote an excellent sonnet in praise of George Crabbe, and it has been frequently assumed that Crabbe may have influenced him. I think that there may be a slight influence of Crabbe, of a very general nature, but it is hard to identify with precision; one should remember that Robinson wrote sonnets also in praise of Zola and of Verlaine and that it would be more than rash to assert that he had been influenced by either one of them. If we use the term *prosaic* in a good sense, the styles of Crabbe and of Robinson may both be said to show a certain prosaic honesty, but there are no devices or mannerisms which are characteristic of both styles, and the narrative methods of the two poets differ widely. Like Crabbe, Robinson had a taste for what one might call the impersonal poem, the poem dealing with his neighbor's experience rather than his own, and especially for the experience of the average villager or small-townsman, but this similarity is of more aid in explaining Robinson's admiration for Crabbe than in proving an influence.

The case of Thomas Hardy is similar. Hardy wrote of the common life of his native region; his outlook was tragic; his style was both plain and powerful; and Robinson admired him. But Robinson does not resemble him except in the very general qualities which I have mentioned. Hardy's best poems are for the most part very brief; even Robinson's short poems run as a rule to several times the length of Hardy's best. Hardy describes the natural landscape in detail and implies the human tragedy. Robinson analyzes the tragedy and implies the landscape. Hardy's poems have the rhythm and the structural characteristics of song, almost of folksong; Robinson's poems have the crisp meter of didactic poetry and the structure of formal exposition.

I have already mentioned that early in his career Robinson showed an interest, which he may have derived from Dr. Schumann, in the early French forms which were practiced around the turn of the century by certain minor British poets, of whom Austin Dobson is the best remembered, forms in which even Swinburne sometimes experimented. About all Robinson shared with the practitioners of these forms, however, was an interest in the forms; within the forms his style shows no particular influence. Among the poems of this kind which he wrote are "Ballade by the Fire," "Ballade of Broken Flutes," "Villanelle of Change" and "The House on the Hill."

Hagedorn tells us that Robinson had a life-long admiration for Kipling, and there occur from time to time in his work poems which might be said to exhibit some influence of Kipling or of the Kiplingesque school, an influence which shows itself in a meter which has something in it of ballad meter even when as occasionally happens it is unrimed, and in a subject matter either too simply dramatic or too simply didactic to appear natural in Robinson. Among the poems which might be listed as showing some trace, though sometimes a vague trace, of such tendencies are "John Evereldown," "The Wilderness," "Stafford's Cabin," "The False Gods" and "London Bridge." With Kipling, as with Crabbe, there is a very general resemblance to Robinson's preference for the clean dry line, to Robinson's general tendency to sacrifice overtone to clarity where sacrifice in either direction seems inescapable, but this is a matter of similarity of taste and hardly of influence.

A more obvious and important influence is that of

Browning. Browning, like Crabbe and Kipling, is a poet who devotes most of his energies to examining the experiences of persons other than himself; but Robinson frequently follows his methods much more closely than he follows those of Crabbe or Kipling. The resemblance is unmistakable in a number of Robinson's dramatic monologues, both in rimed and in blank verse. The method of both poets is to let the character speak for himself, preferably while he is supposedly in the very midst of the experience which he describes. The aim is not only to render and evaluate the experience as an universal one, but to render the character and to render the excitement of the experience while it is actually in process. The first of these aims, which I take to be the most serious of the three for the poet, is inevitably obstructed more or less by the other two. To evaluate an experience truly while one is actually in the midst of it is next to impossible; in such a situation one is in the midst of provisional judgments and rapid impressions and one is distracted by one's own excitement. If the poet is imitating a character in such a situation, this distraction is the essence of his imitation, and the poem tends to devote too much attention to the peripheral and too little to the central. And to render a character by his manner of speaking while in this condition, and by this method only (for we are not concerned here with the expanded and complex form of the true drama) is difficult for the same reason; the poet tends to concentrate on manners of speech rather than on important elements of character, and in the long run the mannerisms are likely to be less those of the character than those of the poet and perhaps even of the method. Browning's "Soliloquy of the

23

Spanish Cloister," for example, is one of his best known poems in this method; it is spoken by a monk in a mood of intense exasperation with one of his brothers:

> Gr-r-r—there go, my heart's abhorrence!
>   Water your damned flower-pots, do!
> If hate killed men, Brother Lawrence,
>   God's blood, would not mine kill you!
> What? your myrtle-bush wants trimming?
>   Oh, that rose has prior claims—
> Needs its leaden vase filled brimming?
>   Hell dry you up with its flames!

Robinson's poem, "The Clinging Vine," is spoken by a jealous wife to her husband, and closely resembles Browning's.

> See the first stanza of "The Cling-ing Vine," page 8, in *Collected Poems* of Edwin Arlington Robinson, New York, The Macmillan Company, 1945. All references to Robinson's poetry will cite this volume, unless otherwise indicated.

The same method is followed in "Ben Jonson Entertains a Man from Stratford." There is a superficial resemblance to Browning's method in many of the long poems, but the resemblance here, I think, as I shall show when I come to them, is largely illusory.

There is an even closer resemblance to the style and method of W. M. Praed, the early nineteenth-century British writer of society verse. This resemblance was first pointed out by the late Professor Hoyt H. Hudson, in one of the most valuable essays which we have upon Robinson and in one of the most perfect demonstrations of an influence made wholly upon the basis of internal evidence with which I am acquainted.[1] There is no external evidence to show that Robinson was acquainted with Praed; Professor Hudson notes this fact, and then calls attention to Praed's poem "The Vicar." "The Vicar" is available in the 1939 edition of *The Oxford Book of English Verse,* and the reader can easily consult the whole poem there at his leisure. I shall quote four of the stanzas to indicate the startling similarity to Robinson's style:

> Some years ago, ere time and taste
>   Had turned our parish topsy-turvy,
> When Darnel Park was Darnel Waste,
>   And roads as little known as scurvy,
> The man who lost his way between
>   St. Mary's Hill and Sandy Thicket,
> Was always shown across the green,
>   And guided to the parson's wicket. . . .
>
> Uprose the Reverend Dr. Brown,
>   Uprose the Doctor's winsome marrow;
> The lady laid her knitting down,
>   Her husband clasp'd his ponderous Barrow;
> Whate'er the stranger's caste or creed,
>   Pundit or Papist, saint or sinner,
> He found a stable for his steed,
>   And welcome for himself, and dinner.
>
> If, when he reached his journey's end,
>   And warmed himself in Court or College,
> He had not gained an honest friend
>   And twenty curious scraps of knowledge,—

[1] The essay is in *Poetry,* February, 1943.

If he departed as he came,
  With no new light on love or liquor,—
Good sooth the traveler was to blame,
  And not the vicarage or the Vicar. . . .

His sermons never said or showed
  That Earth is foul, that Heaven is gracious,
Without refreshment on the road
  From Jerome or from Athanasius:
And sure a righteous zeal inspired
  The hand and head that penn'd and plann'd them,
For all who understood admired,
  And some who did not understand them.

Professor Hudson quotes many passages from both poets
to show the resemblance of manner. I shall have to content
myself with asking the reader to compare, for the moment,
four stanzas of Robinson's "Old King Cole" with the stanzas which I have quoted from Praed.

See "Old King Cole," lines 1-8,
17-24 and 33-48, pages 17-19 in
Collected Poems of Edwin Arlington Robinson.

The poems are alike not only in their metrical form and
in their portrayal of a village character, but in the crisp
statement of easy humor, humor which is for the most part
in fact so easy that it could hardly hope to survive without
the aid of the feminine rimes, and in occasional moments,
such as the last lines of each passage quoted, which offer
a sharper perception or a somewhat more amusing statement and redeem the facility of the whole. A complete

reading of both poems will greatly confirm the impression of similarity.

Of Praed's portrait of Quince, Professor Hudson writes: "After a full-length portrait, Praed presents the death of Quince. The sudden revelation of his long-cherished love, and that accompanied by the gay jests of the doomed man, the whole monologue from the bed, I decided, must have struck Robinson at some time in his youth with such force as to set up in him (or confirm in him) a lasting attitude, a detached and somewhat desperate irony, which marks his most characteristic poetry." Professor Hudson notes that Praed wrote a poem about a man named Clavering, one on a person called Old King Cole, a poem called "Cassandra," and a tribute to Crabbe. "Robinson wrote a sonnet to Thomas Hood; Praed imitated Hood. Praed wrote of Captain Craven and Reuben Nott; Robinson of Captain Craig and Reuben Bright." And he adds: "So far as Robinson caught from Praed an attitude, or temper, he improved upon his source. He moves toward irony where Praed moves toward sentimentality. He analyzes where Praed merely narrated."

The resemblance to Praed is most obvious in Robinson's second-best work, but it can be seen in much of the best. In the great poems, or at least in their greatest stanzas, Robinson achieves a concentration unknown to Praed; but throughout his work he shows a liking for the ingeniously full statement of the small detail, a kind of statement which tends inevitably toward the quality of parlor verse and which may degenerate into mere cleverness. There is, in fact, a close relationship between this kind of verse and

27

the verse which exemplifies the Browning influence. Parlor verse is not invariably written in the parlor, or for it; it is rather an exhibition of the author's cleverness for the benefit of a similarly clever audience, an exhibition made at the expense of the subject; it displays the eccentricities of the personality rather than the centricity of the subject, but always with a large element of humor or irony, and seldom with any other element save a well-controlled sentimentality. Jules Laforgue is the modern classic who may be said most successfully to have taken parlor verse out of the parlor and to have passed it off, more or less, for something else. Robinson sometimes transforms it into something else.

4. THE SHORTER POEMS

1

IN DEALING WITH THE SHORTER POEMS, I SHALL EMPLOY A loose scheme of classification designed to illustrate the aspects of Robinson's thought; it is only in respect to the thought that any particular classification seems necessary. Robinson was not a systematic thinker, and his thought shows conflicting tendencies. I believe that Robinson is essentially a counter-romantic, and yet he resembles other great counter-romantics of the nineteenth and twentieth centuries in the uncritical fashion with which he adopts a few current notions of a romantic nature as if they were axiomatic. One can find such writers as Henry James, Matthew Arnold and Robert Bridges doing much the same thing. There is not any change in Robinson's thinking from the beginning to the end of his work; and if there is any change of emphasis, it is indistinctly perceptible.

2

The evidence of a counter-romantic tendency in Robinson's thinking is to be found easily and repeatedly in his best poems, of which one of the most imposing is "Hillcrest," from *The Man Against the Sky.*

See "Hillcrest," pages 15-17 in
Collected Poems of Robinson.

The setting of the poem, which is dedicated to Mrs. Edward MacDowell, is the MacDowell farmhouse at the Peterborough colony. The place is praised for its isolation and because it is conducive to contemplation. We are told in the first six stanzas that in such a place one may discount one's gains and losses, that one may acquire sufficient humility not to indulge one's own graceful accomplishments or to offer easy consolation to others, and that by contemplation one may learn that one's plans and ideas are often less sound than they sometimes at first appear. The next three stanzas deal with one of Robinson's favorite themes, that of stoical endurance and of the certain necessity for it. In these stanzas and those following, Robinson's style is at something near its greatest; in the second of these three stanzas the visual image, and in the third the abstract statement of the last two lines, are equally impressive. The tenth stanza states the necessity for great wisdom amid the trials of life, and the danger of a little; and the last three stanzas state the illusory nature of a childlike, or romantic, triumph and of the easy assumption of spiritual peace. The phrase "as far as dreams have gone" is perhaps not of the strongest, but the writing in these last stanzas has great strength, and the sensory image of the final stanza has not only extraordinary descriptive beauty but great power of summary. The first six stanzas show less strength than the last seven, but they seem largely successful, both in themselves and as a preparation for what follows. In two lines one sees an indication of one of Robinson's characteristic weaknesses, to which I have alluded in the preceding chapter and to which I shall have to allude more than once again, a tendency to a facile and superficial intellectualism, an intellectualism which is clever rather than perceptive, and which reduces his dry rhythm to the jingling parlor verse which I have described in connection with Praed. In fact, so far as these two lines are concerned, they are too facile not only to be good Robinson but even to be moderately good Praed.

See "Hillcrest," lines 13-14, on page 16 of *Collected Poems* of Robinson.

This kind of thing intrudes, or almost intrudes, too often in Robinson's best work. As a statement of principles, the poem represents a pretty explicit negation of the essential ideas of the romantic movement, especially as that movement has been represented by the Emersonian tradition: it tells us that life is a very trying experience, to be endured only with pain and to be understood only with difficulty; that easy solutions are misleading; that all solutions must be scrutinized; and that understanding is necessary. It is a poem on the tragedy of human life and on the value of

31

contemplation; it expresses neither despair nor triumph, but rather recognition and evaluation.

There are many poems of which the subject is the endurance of suffering, endurance unlightened with hope of anything better. These poems commonly deal with the lives of persons other than the poet, and the subjects offer material for the intellectual examination recommended in "Hillcrest," for the moral curiosity of the heir of the Puritans. Such a poem as "Eros Turannos," for example, puts into practice the principles stated in "Hillcrest"; like "Hillcrest," it is one of Robinson's greatest poems.

See "Eros Turannos," pages 32-33 of *Collected Poems* of Robinson.

This is a universal tragedy in a Maine setting. In the first three stanzas there is an exact definition of the personal motives of the actors and an implication of the social motives; in the fourth stanza the tragic outcome; and in the last two stanzas the generalized commentary. In such a poem we can see to an extraordinary degree the generalizing power of the poetic method; for this piece has the substance of a short novel or of a tragic drama, yet its brevity has resulted in no poverty—its brevity has resulted, rather, in a concentration of meaning and power. In spite of this success, the poem shows in the fifth stanza Robinson's weakness for a kind of provincial cleverness; the paraphrasable substance of the stanza is necessary to the poem, but the statement is undistinguished. Two phrases are especially unfortunate—"tapping on our brows" and "no kindly veil"—but the entire stanza is commonplace. Elsewhere the writing seems to me beyond praise; although it is worth while to call attention especially to the hard and subdued irony of the last lines of the second and third stanzas and to the fact that this irony can enter through the sharp style and metrical form without seeming to intrude into surroundings foreign to it.

I think it worth while to mention a few other poems dealing largely with the theme of endurance, though most of them are less dramatic than "Eros Turannos." Those which I think of first are "Veteran Sirens," "The Poor Relation," "Luke Havergal," "For a Dead Lady" and "Mr. Flood's Party." I could easily add other titles, but these will suffice to illustrate what I have in mind, and they are all among the best poems.

"Veteran Sirens" is an expression of pity for old prostitutes who must continue as best they are able at their trade. It calls to mind Baudelaire's great poem *"Le Jeu,"* but although it is quite as successfully written as Baudelaire's poem, it is far simpler. Baudelaire sees his prostitutes and his gamblers as souls lost through a surrender that has led to automatism, but as having the one surviving virtue of clinging passionately to what life, or, to use the more explicit and theological term, to what being, is left them; and he sees himself as having sunk to a lower level of sin in that he has lost his desire for being. His poem is not a mere lament over suffering and the approach of death, but is a judgment of sin, guided by traditional and theological concepts; it is a judgment upon that way of life which attenuates and diminishes and ultimately abandons what we variously call life, being, or intelligence, in-

33

stead of augmenting it. Robinson's poem is a simple expression of pity at evident suffering, but is stated in the most admirable language.

> See "Veteran Sirens," lines 9-12
> and 17-20 on page 40 of *Collected
> Poems* of Robinson.

"The Poor Relation" describes an old woman, presumably of good family, living in loneliness and in poverty. The first seven stanzas of this poem give the effect of some redundancy; what they have to say is simple and could be said in less space. Furthermore, a fair number of lines are saved from sentimentality, if indeed they are saved, only by the clipped intricacy of the stanza and the hardness of the meter.

> See "The Poor Relation," lines 7-
> 8 on page 45 and lines 9-10 and
> 21-22 on page 46 of *Collected
> Poems* of Robinson.

In the eighth stanza, however, the poem is drawn together by the old woman's vision of the city, in one of the greatest triumphs of Robinson's rhetoric.

> See "The Poor Relation," lines 1-
> 8 on page 47 of *Collected Poems*
> of Robinson.

The simile of the last two lines of this stanza is one of the few successful comparisons in literature between the vis-
34

ual and the auditory, the success being made possible by the fact that the two items have a common ground for comparison in the *rhythm* of their movements. The secondary levels of the Imagist movement, the work of Amy Lowell and of J. G. Fletcher, for example, abounded in comparisons of sounds with colors, comparisons which in their nature are arbitrary and meaningless; but Robinson's comparison has life because it is founded in reality. The last stanza, which is admirable throughout, contains two lines which seem to me finer, perhaps, than anything else in the poem.

> See "The Poor Relation," lines 11-
> 12 on page 47 of *Collected Poems*
> of Robinson.

This bare statement of perfect tragedy seems to me beyond improvement. It is not Emersonian, nor is it the work of an Emersonian.

"Luke Havergal" is less simple in its subject than are the last two poems which I have mentioned, and it illustrates less purely the theme of simple endurance. The poem is an address to Luke Havergal, spoken, apparently, by the woman whom he had loved, from beyond the grave; or at any rate such is his illusion. He is told that he may find her through suicide. It might be said, I presume, that the poem seems to display a faith in life after death; but if one considers the intense desolation of the tone, it becomes rather an expression of longing for death, of inability to endure more.

35

See "Luke Havergal," lines 9-16
on page 74 of *Collected Poems*
of Robinson.

"For a Dead Lady" is an elegy unlightened by any miti-
gating idea or feeling; it is purely a lament for the dead.
Robinson suggests no way of dealing with the experience
except that we understand it and endure it.

See "For a Dead Lady," lines 17-
24 on page 355 of *Collected
Poems* of Robinson.

"Mr. Flood's Party" is less compact than most of these
poems, and it is written with a kind of compassionate humor, but the same theme of irremediable tragedy governs
it.

"The Wandering Jew" is a few years later than any poem
I have thus far mentioned except the last. It is certainly
one of the greatest of Robinson's short poems, perhaps the
greatest; it comes closer to complete success than most.
It is an interesting poem for certain incidental reasons as
well. Although most of Robinson's great poems contain
very little sensory imagery, this poem contains less than
most; it is almost purely a poetry of ideas. Yet the ideas
arise from the consideration of the particular case; the
case is not used to illustrate the ideas. That is, the poem is
not what we would call a didactic or philosophic poem.
Except in "Hillcrest," Robinson probably never succeeds
very brilliantly with the didactic or philosophical, whereas
he often succeeds brilliantly with the poem of the particular case. It is curious to see a poet handle "abstract" lan-

guage so brilliantly as in this poem and in "Eros Turannos" and so ineptly as in "The Man Against the Sky" and certain other poems which I shall discuss later in this chapter. He *thinks* well here; he does other things well likewise—but he thinks well and intricately; in "The Man Against the Sky" he thinks badly. But what I want to point out above all is this: that in a period which is convinced that thought and poetry are mutually destructive, that rational structure is a defect in a poem rather than a virtue, that genuine poetry must be confused to express a confused period, that poetry is primarily sensory and depends for its strength upon large quantities of sensory imagery, Robinson has written a poem (to mention only this one) which is rational in general structure, packed with thought in its detail, perfectly clear in its meaning and development, and nearly free from sensory imagery, and that this poem is one of the great poems not only of our time but of our language.

See "The Wandering Jew," pages
456-459 in *Collected Poems* of
Robinson.

It is interesting to observe here the complete transmutation of the method of Praed's poem "The Vicar" and of Robinson's "Old King Cole" into something deeply serious. The feminine rimes of those poems, with their excessive emphasis on neatness, have been abandoned; in fact the number of rimes has been reduced to half, with the result that the precision of statement, though it is undiminished, is muted and unobtrusive. The same method of extremely careful definition of shades of meaning is employed; but in those poems the meanings were slight to the point of triviality, and the care resulted in cleverness; in this poem the meanings are profound, and the care results in a power which has seldom been equaled. I can only recommend a careful study of this poem, a study concentrated especially upon the last five stanzas, in which the force of the statement begins to accumulate. To cite excerpts is perhaps foolish, for the language is quiet and its effectiveness depends upon its place in the context; nevertheless, the isolation of a few passages may help the reader to observe the quality which I have in mind. The last two lines of the third stanza are a remarkably fine statement of an acute though limited insight. The last two lines of the fourth stanza have a similar virtue. But it is the later stanzas, in which the central theme is developed, which offer the most powerful passages.

See "The Wandering Jew," lines
12-17 and 24-25 on page 458 of
Collected Poems of Robinson.

This is very great poetry, perhaps as great as one can easily find. I do not wish to labor the point unnecessarily, but there is a common inability in our time to distinguish between poetry written in plain and generalized diction and poetry which is dull or even trite; it is essential that the distinction be made.

The poem should not be construed, I think, as an attempt to evaluate Jewish character, if such an entity may be said to exist; it is rather an attempt to examine a spiritual vice which may occur in any group at a fairly high intellectual and spiritual level. The vice is the vice of pride in one's own identity, a pride which will not allow one to accept a greater wisdom from without even when one recognizes that the wisdom is there and is greater than one's own; the result is spiritual sickness. The Wandering Jew is simply a mythological figure who embodies this vice in a useable form. This meaning is pointed repeatedly and sharply in the last stanzas, and finally in the last two lines of the poem.

Three of Robinson's later sonnets seem to me among the greatest of his works: "Lost Anchors," "Many Are Called," and "The Sheaves." In fact if one adds to these sonnets and "The Wandering Jew" two or three of the blank verse monologues—"The Three Taverns," "Rembrandt to Rembrandt," and perhaps "John Brown"—one probably has Robinson at his greatest.

"Lost Anchors" is a commentary on the conversation of an old sailor; the sailor is not of great importance in himself, but he is made a symbol of the immeasurable antiquity of the sea and of its ruins.

See "Lost Anchors" on pages 577-578 of *Collected Poems* of Robinson.

The poem is wholly admirable, but the skill with which the sailor's illegitimate birth, mentioned, as it is, at the very end, is made to imply the amoral and archaic nature of the sea, is something which can scarcely be too long pondered or too greatly admired.

"Many Are Called" is a sonnet on the rarity of poetic genius and the loneliness of its reward.

See "Many Are Called" on pages
581-582 of *Collected Poems* of
Robinson.

The second half of the octave displays a characteristic form of Robinson's irony, and the sixth line follows in a measure a familiar Victorian formula which the Fowlers have described,[1] of which the procedure is to relate disparate elements in a parallel construction, with the intention of startling. Robinson's line is a curious variant, however. The word *vain* in English is in almost every expression an adjective, coming from the Latin *vanus,* so that we feel vaguely in using this expression, *in vain,* that a subsequent noun is somehow understood; or perhaps the fixed form of the expression gives us the sense of a single adverb instead of the sense of an adverbial phrase; and to the extent that we have either feeling, we get the impression that the phrase *in vain* is not parallel grammatically with the two phrases preceding, but is parallel only in superficial appearance. Since the word *vain* in this expression is derived from the substantive *vanum,* however, the three phrases are actually parallel in construction, and any such feeling which one may have is delusive, yet I suspect that Robinson desired to invoke such a feeling. The real divergence from parallelism is not in the grammar

[1] H. W. and F. G. Fowler, *The King's English,* p. 182, in the chapter entitled "Airs and Graces." Among the examples listed are: ". . . they return together in triumph and a motor-car" (*Times*); "Miss Nipper . . . shook her head and a tin-cannister" (Dickens).

but in the sense, for the first two phrases relate to states of mind, and the third to an end. In the passages cited by the Fowlers, the humor resides in a descent from the heroic to the prosaic, or in a shift from the natural to the ridiculous. But the irony in this case is spiritual; Robinson means each one of his items seriously, and the irony is the tragic irony of frustration. The risk involved in the use of any such formula is great, but the passage appears successful. And such rhetorical device, no matter how stereotyped, may be used successfully if it is used deliberately and with adequate motive by a poet of ability, as a study of the puns and other plays upon words in the English poets of the Renaissance will fully demonstrate.[2] The irony is quiet, and to some extent the formulary statement of it keeps it quiet; and the quietness permits the poem to return easily to the high seriousness of the sestet and even to return with a certain intensification of that seriousness. These four lines might easily have slipped into the superficial cleverness of which Robinson is so often guilty; they represent a successful handling of what he apparently tries and fails to do in other passages to which I have already called attention.

"The Sheaves" employs a descriptive technique to symbolize the impenetrable mystery of the physical universe

[2] See for example "A Farewell," one of the greatest sonnets by Sidney, with its tireless play upon *part, depart* and *impart;* Shakespeare's "Golden lads and girls all must/ As chimney-sweepers, come to dust"; and Donne's "Thy Grace may wing me to prevent his art/ And Thou, like adamant, draw mine iron heart." One can find innumerable other puns and plays upon words in the period, and even in Shakespeare, which are very bad; but they are bad because the formula is badly managed or badly inspired, not because the formula is employed.

as seen at any moment and the mystery of the fact of change.

See "The Sheaves" on pages 870-871 of *Collected Poems* of Robinson.

3

There is another aspect of Robinson which I must discuss briefly—his obscurity. Much of Robinson was found obscure by his earlier readers, and for the most part as a result of their own indolence or ignorance, and the term "mysticism" was frequently employed to describe the obscurity; I take it that the word was used as a polite form of disapproval and was not intended seriously, for whatever there is or is not in Robinson's verse, there is no mysticism.[3] There has been a great deal of obscurity in modern

[3] The mystic, traditionally considered, is one who experiences occasionally and briefly a direct communion with God, a communion which is supra-rational and incommensurate with normal human experience, so that it cannot properly be described in language. The discipline of the mystic is a religious and moral discipline which prepares him for this experience. Mystical poetry deals either with the experience itself, but imperfectly and by way of some human analogy, or with the discipline. According to the Catholic doctrine, the mystical experience is granted to very few persons and is not a necessary part of the religious life. Calvinistic and related Protestant doctrine, however, tends to identify the mystical experience with the operation of Grace and to make it a necessary part of the religious life, and to identify both with "conscience," which thus becomes an inexplicable feeling instead of right reason, with which Catholic doctrine identifies conscience. Emerson, with his pantheistic doctrine, identified God with his creation, impulse with conscience, and surrender to impulse with the mystical experience.

verse, and where it has not been due merely to incompetent writing, it has been mainly of two kinds. Sometimes the poet endeavors to be perfectly lucid, but he thinks so badly that he makes statements which are without his realizing it incomprehensible. Such statements in modern American verse belong most frequently to the tradition of Emerson and Whitman, and there are a few mild examples of this kind of obscurity in Robinson, examples to which I shall eventually refer. When Emerson, in "The Problem," tells us that the artist produces art unconsciously, functioning as a divinely controlled automaton, we cannot understand him, because we can imagine an automaton only as a madman; the statement is unbelievable and unimaginable. When Hart Crane, in "The Dance," describes under veils of metaphor the apotheosis of Maquokeeta as union with the American soil, we are similarly baffled, for a man cannot be imagined as both keeping and losing his personal identity. Sometimes, however, the poet may be fully conscious that he is obscure; he may follow the example of the later Mallarmé and suppress the rational element in his poems in the mistaken idea that he is thus strengthening the emotional; or he may write as it would seem that Rimbaud frequently wrote, more or less automatically, in a state more or less approximating hallucination, with the mistaken idea (one which Emerson shared without putting it into practice) that the automatic is of necessity divinely inspired, thus achieving fantastic symbols with the empty semblance only of significance, symbols arranged in a meaningless sequence.[4] Reference to strange bits of eru-

[4] This describes most of Rimbaud's poems in prose and some but not all of those in verse. There is much else that one could say of

43

dition, such as we get in Pound, may cause temporary obscurity, but only till an appropriate doctoral dissertation may be written; and this is true likewise of reference to a private set of symbols, such as we get in Blake. The method of progression by revery, or random association, which we get in Pound's *Cantos*, may seem to result in obscurity, but only if one fails to recognize the method and is expecting to disentangle something which was never there.[5]

Robinson's commonest form of obscurity, I should judge, has no relationship to any of these varieties. His esthetic is not Mallarméan, his philosophy is a matter of relatively simple common sense, and the themes of such of his obscure poems as I have been able to understand are anything but profound. But there is a kind of New Englander, of which Robinson is a belated and somewhat attenuated example, in which ingenuity has become a form of eccentricity; when you encounter a gentleman of this breed, you cannot avoid feeling that he may at any moment sit down on the rug and begin inventing a watch or a conundrum. Franklin and the first O. W. Holmes were specimens of the ingenious Yankee at his best; Henry Adams with his theory of history is in part a specimen of the ingenious Yankee gone wrong; and Robinson in a few of his poems is a specimen of the ingenious Yankee become whimsical.

The method of the obscure poems is best introduced by a poem which does not quite succeed in becoming obscure

---

Rimbaud, a good deal of it in his favor, but this is his chief defect, and heaven knows it is sufficiently serious.

[5] These matters are discussed in a good deal of detail in my book entitled *Primitivism and Decadence*, Arrow Editions, New York, 1937.

and in which one can therefore see plainly how the method works. The poem is "The Mill" from *The Three Taverns.*

See "The Mill" on pages 460-461
of *Collected Poems* of Robinson.

We learn in the first stanza that the miller's wife has forebodings because her husband has left her with an expression of discouragement at the disappearance of his trade; in the second stanza that her husband has hanged himself; and in the third stanza that she drowns herself in the millstream; yet all this is stated with a certain amount of indirectness, though not with enough to obscure the meaning. In the poem "The Whip," the method results in more difficulty. I suggest that the reader examine it carefully at least two or three times, before proceeding to my comment, to see if he can deduce the meaning.

See "The Whip" on pages 338-
339 of *Collected Poems* of Robinson.

The indirection of statement, aided by what one might call a more or less metaphysical tone, results in pretty successful obscurity; one suspects a concealed symbolism, dealing with a more or less general theme—or at least I did so for a number of years, although my obtuseness now strikes me as somewhat curious.[6] The poem actually deals with a brutal melodrama, of a kind of which Robinson was es-

[6] For my paraphrase of this poem I am indebted to Mr. Don Stanford.

45

pecially fond,[7] and of which "The Mill" is a rather mild
specimen. We are given a man and wife and the wife's
lover. The husband had long suspected his wife's fidelity,
but had fought the suspicion. The three are in some fashion
tipped out from a boat in a river, perhaps from the same
boat, perhaps, as the fifth line of the fourth stanza suggests, from two boats, or at any rate with the husband in
some way in pursuit of the two others. As the three are
about to emerge to safety, the wife turns and strikes her
husband across the face; and recognizing the certainty of
what he had before suspected, he chooses to sink rather
than save himself and face his tragedy. All of the necessary
information is given us in pretty clear statements; but it
is given fragmentarily, and interspersed with comments
which are likely to be misleading, and in a tone which is
misleading. As a conclusion to this topic, I wish to cite a
sonnet for which I am unable to offer an explanation but
which I suspect to be a highly successful experiment in the
same kind of procedure. It is called "En Passant."

See "En Passant" on pages 886-
887 of *Collected Poems* of Robinson.

4

There are a good many poems which deal with the subject of God and immortality, but they are not remarkably
clear. The most ambitious of these is "The Man Against

[7] See, for example, "Aaron Stark," "Reuben Bright," "The Tavern" and "Haunted House"; and among the longer poems *Cavender's House.*

the Sky," a fairly long contemplative poem, of which the versification is generally similar to that of "Dover Beach." The poem opens with a description of a solitary man crossing a hilltop into the sunset. This man is symbolic of man in general approaching death. Robinson says that his symbolic man may have progressed through great anguish to a triumphant death; or that he may have proceeded easily in the light of an uncritical faith; or that he may have been disillusioned, a stoical artist or philosopher, passing indifferently to extinction; or that he may have been disappointed in life and fearfully unreconciled to death; or that he may have been a mechanistic philosopher, proud of an intellectual construction which gave him no personal hope; but in any event that he represents all of us in that he approaches death alone, to face it as he is able. Robinson asks, then, whether we may not have some expectation of a future life, even if we doubt the existence of Heaven and Hell; and why, if we believe in Oblivion, we are guilty of perpetuating the race. He replies that we know, "if we know anything," the existence of a Deity, a Word, which we perceive fragmentarily and imperfectly, and that this knowledge is our sole justification for not ending ourselves and our kind.

See "The Man Against the Sky," lines 26-32 on page 66 of *Collected Poems* of Robinson.

The nature of this Deity, and the nature of our knowledge, are not defined further than this; the crux of the poem is thus offered briefly and vaguely in a few lines; and the greater part of the concluding section is devoted to describing the desolation which we should experience without this knowledge. Philosophically, the poem is unimpressive; stylistically, it is all quite as weak as the lines referred to above; and structurally, it seems to defeat its purpose— for while it purports to be an expression of faith, it is devoted in all save these same few lines to the expression of despair.

"Credo," from *Children of the Night*, perhaps expresses a similar concept and in an equally unsatisfactory manner, but the connective *for* which introduces the second half of the sestet is confusing.

> See "Credo" on page 94 of *Collected Poems* of Robinson.

In a "Sonnet," from the same collection, there is a statement of belief in God based on the evidence of human love and the beauty of nature; this, as far as it goes, might be Christian or Emersonian or neither.

> See "Sonnet" on page 96 of *Collected Poems* of Robinson.

I do not mention these poems for their poetic virtue, for they have little; the language is vague and trite, the fifth line of the poem just noted is rhythmically very flat and is guilty of a needless and clumsy use of the progressive form of the verb, and Belshazzar's wall is a curious place on which to read the glory of eternal partnership. But the poems are characteristic expressions of this phase of Robinson's thought; they are characteristic, in fact, of his efforts to express generalized thought of any variety; and they may perhaps serve as some justification of my failure to come to definite conclusions with regard to the precise form of Robinson's theology.

In the "Octaves," from the same collection, we have a sequence of poems for the most part on the experiential evidence for a belief in God; the evidence is defined very vaguely, in spite of the effort to achieve a gnomic style, but the writing in certain lines achieves a strength greater than any in the three poems which I have just been discussing. The ninth of these is clearer than most; it deals with the disappointment which we feel when a person of high character displays weakness, and the disappointment is offered as evidence of the real existence of the impersonal standard.

> See "Octaves," lines 7-14 on page
> 103 of *Collected Poems* of Rob-
> inson.

The poem illustrates a defect very obvious throughout the group of which it is a part, and often evident elsewhere in Robinson. The movement is stiff and insensitive—Robinson's ear is in gereral so deficient that he usually needs the support of rime and of a compact form—and the lines read as if they ought to be rimed and were left unrimed through an oversight. The lines stop so emphatically at the ends that the expression *on earth*, at the beginning of the sixth line, has the effect of an awkward afterthought, and its redundancy is made obvious. The eleventh octave is one of the best written, but offers no solution to the prob-

lem posed; it deals merely with the unsatisfied search for
the solution.

See "Octaves," lines 23-26 on page
103 and lines 1-4 on page 104 of
Collected Poems of Robinson.

The language applied in these poems to the evidence for a
belief in God, language, for example, like "spirit-gleams
of Wisdom" in the eighth, is likely to be both vague and
more or less romantic in its connotations; such a phrase as
the one just quoted, in fact, would perhaps appear to indicate a belief in the discovery of God through pure intuition and lend some support to those who find a strong
trace of Emerson in Robinson; but there is not sufficient
evidence in the poems to prove that the intuition is Emersonian intuition or that the God is Emerson's God, and
there is explicit contrary evidence elsewhere. The worst
one can say of the poems is that in general they are carelessly thought and carelessly written. Emerson used language reminiscent of Edwards without being a Christian; [8]
Robinson could easily have used language reminiscent of
Emerson without having been an Emersonian. Robinson,
especially in his earlier years, might well have resembled
a good many learned scholars of my acquaintance who
claim to admire Emerson and who quote him by phrases,
but who fail to understand or for sentimental reasons re-

[8] See "Jonathan Edwards to Emerson," by Perry Miller, *The New
England Quarterly*, XIII-4. See also the essays called "The Puritan
Heresy" and "Emerson," *The Hound and Horn*, Vol. V, and re-
printed in *The Pragmatic Test*, by H. B. Parkes. The Colt Press,
San Francisco.

fuse to admit the total effect of his work. This kind of thing is fairly common and seems merely to indicate a normal and healthy capacity on the part of superior minds. "The Sage" appears to be a poem in praise of Emerson, but it does not define his doctrine. One could adduce a little more evidence of this kind from the shorter poems, but I believe that all of it would be similarly inconclusive.

5

Aside from explicit expressions of theory, however, there are occasional indications of a romantic attitude in Robinson, an attitude belonging especially to the 1890's, the period of his youth. "Flammonde" will do as an example. The poem praises an individual whom one might characterize as the sensitive parasite or as the literary or academic sponge.

> See "Flammonde," lines 9-16 on
> page 3 and lines 12-19 on page 4
> of *Collected Poems* of Robinson.

Now the near-genius of this kind, who represents an especially unfortunate type of failure, and who is frequently, as in the case of Flammonde, a somewhat unpleasant specimen, obsessed Robinson throughout his life for reasons which were largely personal. Frequently the poverty in which he lived threw him into the company of such people, and he may at times have visualized himself as one of them, though he could scarcely have visualized himself as Flammonde. But this obsession is not in itself an explanation of the language which Robinson uses, language which is reminiscent of the worst sentimentalism of the nineties, or even of lachrymose popular balladry.

> See "Flammonde," lines 20-23
> and 28-30 on page 4 and lines 13-
> 14 on page 6 of *Collected Poems*
> of Robinson.

The classicism, the precision, of Robinson's great work is not in this poem; there is nothing here of it but an empty mannerism. The substance as a whole and phrase by phrase is repulsively sentimental. Yet the poem has been repeatedly offered as one of Robinson's great achievements; it perhaps comes as close to the classical as the average critic of our time is able to follow. In "Richard Cory," another favorite, we have a superficially neat portrait of the elegant man of mystery; the poem builds up deliberately to a very cheap surprise ending; but all surprise endings are cheap in poetry, if not, indeed, elsewhere, for poetry is written to be read not once but many times. Such poems, however, although there are more like them, are relatively rare.

6

Robinson wrote a small but definite group of poems dealing with his political and social ideas, and although some of them are of greater length than the other poems discussed in this chapter, I shall take them up here for the sake of convenience. Most of these poems are poor and none are of his best; in general, they indicate the abilities and disabilities to which I have already pointed: the best adhere most closely to the case of the individual man, the worst adventure farthest into general theory. I have in mind "The Master," "The Revealer," "Cassandra," "Demos," "On the Way," "Dionysus in Doubt," and "Demos and Dionysus."

"The Master," a poem on Lincoln, and "The Revealer," a poem on Theodore Roosevelt, are primarily poems in praise of their respective subjects; but they indicate, perhaps not very clearly, Robinson's distrust of the common man and his belief in the superior leader as the only hope for democracy. They are the best poems in this group, "The Master" especially standing well up among the best of Robinson's secondary poems. "Cassandra" is a poem warning the nation against the naively enthusiastic commercialism of the early part of this century.

> See "Cassandra," lines 9-12 on
> page 12 of *Collected Poems* of
> Robinson.

The admirable sharpness of such satirical statements as this is not equaled by his statements in praise of the virtues which he defends.

> See "Cassandra," lines 20-28 on
> page 12 of *Collected Poems* of
> Robinson.

He does not tell us what old verities he has in mind nor how old they are—whether, for example, they are the verities of Emerson or those of Aquinas. Nor does he define the

53

nature of the price in the last stanza, and a good many divergent definitions would be possible. He is quite as vague here as in his references to a positive theology; yet the force of a didactic poem depends precisely upon the clarity and validity of the ideas expressed.

"Demos," a double sonnet, warns us that "the few shall save the many, or the many are to fall"; but Robinson is again too vague. Does he mean, for example, that democracy cannot survive unless it is regularly governed by great men? If so, there is small hope for it, for great men rise to power in a democracy only occasionally and as a result of their being incidentally great politicians or as a result of some other chance. Robinson may mean that the common mass should be improved little by little by the teachings of great men as those teachings after many years reach them and become a part of tradition. I should place my own modest hopes in this latter formula, and in the belief that for the immediate present the common man is guided in some measure by such traditional wisdom, imperfectly as he may apprehend it and profit by it, and by a fairly acute sense of where the economic and social shoe pinches; this is not the formula for an Utopia, but I think it works reasonably well. But Robinson, unfortunately, does not say what he means, and he seems at times to be recommending a Carlylean leader-worship, or a doctrine of an elite class, either of which in practice would result in a Hitler or in an oligarchy.

"On the Way" is a dialogue spoken by Hamilton and Burr at a time when they were still superficially friendly with each other. Burr expresses the personal jealousy of a politician for a man greater than himself—that is, Washington—and Hamilton expresses an admiration for Washington similar to that expressed elsewhere by Robinson for Lincoln and Theodore Roosevelt.

See "On the Way," lines 24-30 on page 480 and lines 1-10 on page 481 of *Collected Poems* of Robinson.

With the admiration for Washington one cannot quarrel, nor can one quarrel with the unkind but essentially true statements about the common man; but again one is at a loss to discern the relationship of Washington to the common man, the way in which he may be said to guide the common man or be of value to him. In the nature of this relationship lies all the difference between barbarism and civilization, however halting. For Washington will be merely a menace to the nation if the common man depends upon him blindly. Unless the influence of Washington can outlast Washington, can teach the common man a few truths and give him a few perceptions, so that he can hope to survive the intervals between Washingtons, then the common man is lost.

"Dionysus in Doubt" deals immediately with the Prohibition Amendment of the 1920's, but more generally with the impropriety of legislation upon questions which are matters of personal morality rather than public.

See "Dionysus in Doubt," line 34 on page 860 and lines 1-6 on page 861 of *Collected Poems* of Robinson.

With this as a starting point, he deals sketchily with common personal attitudes which he finds a menace to society.

See "Dionysus in Doubt," lines
10-26 on page 865 of *Collected
Poems* of Robinson.

These attitudes, and others which he attacks, are, as he says, a danger; but they are no more common and no more dangerous in democracies than elsewhere. Robinson appears to have confused the vices of humanity with the vices of his country. The writing, moreover, is lax and indolent, whereas satiric and didactic poetry should be compact and sharp; the confusing of the trite figure of the watchdog with the equally trite figure of the dog in a manger is an especially bad example of this laxness. Dionysus goes on to meditate on the dangers of the standardization of the human mind implicit in the kind of legislation to which he is objecting.

See "Dionysus in Doubt," lines
20-26 on page 866 of *Collected
Poems* of Robinson.

But once more Robinson seems to read into his own age and country a danger common to all times and countries: Socrates, Galileo, Abelard and Columbus suffered from this vice in human nature no less surely than anyone has done more recently. The tendency for the mediocre norm to impose itself and for the superior individual to combat and escape this norm or to be sacrificed to it have always existed and I imagine always will; and as for the Prohibition Amendment, we eventually got rid of it. I have no objection to the castigation of vices, and the vices which Robinson castigates are real; but unless they are rightly located, the poem suffers and there is the possibility that society may suffer. The reader may assume, for example, that there was less standardization and more individual freedom under Louis XIV of France or Phillip II of Spain; but although the reigns of those monarchs may have been marked by important values which we lack, yet freedom was not one of them, and it strikes me as doubtful that the values in question would be recovered by the re-establishment of comparable political systems. Before we blame our spiritual defects on a political system which it has cost blood and centuries to establish, merely because the defects and the system coincide in time, we would do well to make a careful study of historical causes. And this issue is not irrelevant to the question of poetry; a poem which embodies so careless an outburst is not an adult performance—that is, it is not a good poem. "Demos and Dionysus" develops much the same argument, and with no greater distinction.

7

In conclusion, I shall repeat that nearly all of Robinson's best poems appear to deal with particular persons and situations; in these poems his examination is careful and intelligent, his method is analytic, and his style is mainly very distinguished. If we are to risk pushing historical influences for all they are worth, we may say that in such poems Rob-

inson exhibits the New England taste for practical morality, a passionate curiosity about individual dramas, and
that in examining them he is guided by the moral and spiritual values of the general Christian tradition as they have
come down to him in the form of folk wisdom or common
sense, although in the application of these values he shows
a penetration and subtlety which are the measure of his
genius. In his more generalized, or philosophic, poems, he
is almost always careless in his thinking and equally careless in his style, and it is in these poems that one may see—
often in the method and sometimes in the form of the
thought—the influence of Emersonian romanticism. "Hillcrest" is the most notable exception to this last statement.

Robinson is thus a poet whose thought is incomplete
and in a measure contradictory; he would have been a
greater poet had this not been so, but we should remember
that he is no worse in this respect than Wordsworth, Hardy,
Arnold or Bridges, if indeed he be as bad. Furthermore,
within certain definitely delimited areas during the greater
part of his career, his approach to his material is sound; we
have seen this approach defined in "Hillcrest" and practiced in a number of other poems. The approach is what
we may call critical and rationalistic; and the poetry is
reasoning poetry. It is true that reasoning poetry has often
been written to attack the reason—Pope's *Essay on Man*
and most of Emerson may serve as examples—but these
poems by Robinson are not written to attack the reason,
they are written to illustrate it. It is an extremely careful
poetry. I do not mean this in any superficial sense; I mean
that Robinson not only scrutinizes his thought but also is
watchful of his feeling. His New England heritage here is

58

not a defect, even though he chooses occasionally to ridicule it; the feeling which *ought* to be motivated by his comprehension of the matter is what he seeks to express—he is not simply on a tour in search of emotion. And since his matter is often important and his comprehension sometimes profound, this exact adjustment of feeling to motive results on certain occasions in poetry of extremely great value.

The greatest poems, not all of which achieve perfection, are probably the following: from *The Children of the Night* (1890–97), "Luke Havergal" and "The Clerks"; from *Captain Craig, Etc.* (1902), none; from *The Town Down the River* (1910), "For a Dead Lady"; from *The Man Against the Sky* (1916), "Hillcrest," "Eros Turannos," "Veteran Sirens" and "The Poor Relation"; from *The Three Taverns* (1920), "The Wandering Jew"; from *Avon's Harvest, Etc.* (1921), "Lost Anchors" and "Many Are Called"; from *Dionysus in Doubt* (1925), "The Sheaves." After this there is only one volume, *Nicodemus* (1932), containing any short poems, and that contains only a few and none of importance. These eleven poems can be equaled, I think, in the work of only four or five English and American poets of the past century and a half.

To list all of the secondary poems of importance would be tedious and might lead to a number of unduly fine decisions, but I offer an incomplete list of my favorites as an introductory guide to the reader who may not be familiar with Robinson; this list alone, I suspect, would suffice to give Robinson a permanent reputation, had he done nothing better: from *Children of the Night*, "Horace to Leuconoë" and "George Crabbe"; from *Captain Craig, Etc.*,

"The Growth of Lorraine"; from *The Town Down the River*, "The Master," "The White Lights," "Doctor of Billiards," "Miniver Cheevy" and "Two Gardens in Linndale"; from *The Man Against the Sky*, "Another Dark Lady" and "The Voice of the Age"; from *The Three Taverns*, "The Valley of the Shadow," "The Mill," "Dark Hills" and "Souvenir"; from *Avon's Harvest, Etc.*, "Mr. Flood's Party," "Vain Gratuities" and "The Long Race"; from *Dionysus in Doubt*, "The Haunted House," "Karma," "New England," "Reunion," "A Christmas Sonnet."

I have not listed any of the Browningesque monologues and dialogues, such as "The Clinging Vine" and "John Gorham," poems which have no doubt contributed heavily to Robinson's popularity; for reasons which I have given elsewhere, these do not impress me as being serious poetry, and I have tried to select poems more concentrated and less obviously derivative. It should be remembered that these selections are from the shorter works only; not even the poems of moderate length, such as "The Three Taverns," have been considered—I shall deal with these in one of my last chapters.

5. THE THREE ARTHURIAN POEMS

1

OF THE THREE ARTHURIAN POEMS, *MERLIN* AND *LANCELOT* contain the best poetry—in fact, they contain the best poetry to be found in Robinson's longer works, regardless of subject; *Lancelot*, moreover, is the best constructed of Robinson's longer poems and strikes me as one of the most powerfully constructed long poems in English; *Tristram*, though far inferior in both respects, is probably better than nearly any other long poem by Robinson. It is interesting, with respect to the action, that *Lancelot* adheres very closely to the plot which one finds scattered loosely through Malory, although the integration and interpretation of the action, and the characterization, are Robinson's own, and that in both *Merlin* and *Tristram* Robinson indulges in a good deal of invention, suppression and alteration, no matter which of the earlier treatments one examines. These changes are responsible for the weak structure of *Merlin* and likewise for the extraordinary symbolic power of some

61

of its concluding passages; they are responsible for the serious enfeeblement of *Tristram*. Robinson's uses and alterations of his original texts would be a subject more proper to a master's thesis than to the present essay; I shall mention them only as they affect the success of his poems.

I do not wish to be more tedious than necessary, but I shall indulge in summaries, many of them detailed, of most of the longer poems. There are two or three reasons for doing this. In the first place, Robinson's method of telling a story is frequently too ingeniously indirect for comfort, so that unless one starts with a summary, one is normally forced to read the poem through for the express purpose of making one before one can begin to consider the values of the poem as a whole. In the second place, much of the value of a long poem is closely related to the action, and such value cannot be discussed unless the action is held more or less clearly in mind. Where the non-Arthurian poems are concerned, there is, unfortunately, an additional reason: it is only by seeing the plots in close juxtaposition that one can adequately observe the formula which Robinson usually employed and the weakness of the formula, and few readers will ever have the patience to read the entire series in a short enough space of time to hold the plots clearly in mind and compare them.

2

Merlin was published in 1917, and except for "Captain Craig," is the earliest poem by Robinson of more than medium length; and it is the first attempt at what one might call a formal narrative. Merlin himself is conceived not as an aged and mysterious magician such as we find in Malory, not as a senile and incredible stock figure such as we find in Tennyson and find parodied in Mark Twain, but as an extremely intelligent man in middle age, at the height of great mental and physical power, who is adviser to the king not because he is incapable of being a knight but because he is capable of more important work. His prophetic power appears to be mainly the clear foresight of great intelligence, but it is given a supernatural air by the fatalism which is central to the theme. Merlin perceives that, given certain men of great force and limited understanding in certain initial situations, certain disasters are virtually inescapable. The poem deals with two actions, which are only loosely connected: on the one hand Merlin's love affair with Vivian, and on the other the disintegration of Arthur's kingdom. The first of these is handled ingeniously and sometimes charmingly, but it is not in itself extremely impressive; the second is seen as a spectacle, and in its last stages, and it is not seen as a drama, and the chief power of the poem resides in the commentary, largely through the mind of Merlin, on the spectacle. The actions are connected only to this extent, that Merlin's love for Vivian prevents his coming to Arthur's aid until too late, yet the real theme of the poem is that the catastrophe was inevitable and that no help would have availed. There is, then, no real causative relation of the one part to the other, though conversely Merlin's distress over Arthur's situation brings about the end of his relations with Vivian. The situation between Merlin and Vivian is dramatic as far as it goes, but it is of secondary interest in the poem; the main interest for us, as for Robinson, is the spectacle of Arthur's downfall, but this, so far as the structure of the entire poem goes, merely provides a frame for the love story.

In the first section, Gawaine and Dagonet talk of the rumor that Merlin has returned from his "living grave" in Broceliande. Gawaine, here as in *Lancelot*, is conceived as the graceful, intense and mercurial figure of Malory and of Tennyson; but Dagonet is a mature man, frail, neurotic, witty and tragic, yet neither a child nor a fool. Gawaine and Dagonet talk indirectly of the dangers hovering over Camelot, neither quite trusting the other. In the second section Lamorak and Bedivere discuss the same subject, speaking more frankly of Lancelot and Guinevere, and of Arthur's bastard son, Modred,[1] who wants both the kingdom and Guinevere. They are represented as men of great strength, both physical and moral, Bedivere having by far the greater intellectual penetration. Kay joins the conversation but remains a somewhat unimpressive figure. In the third section, Arthur and Merlin talk. Merlin says that dire trouble for Arthur is near at hand; he says that it is Modred, not Lancelot, who is Arthur's real enemy, although there is no help for the love of Lancelot and Guinevere. He advises the king to leave the queen to Lancelot

---

[1] Robinson follows Malory and earlier writers here, in making Modred the son of Arthur by his sister, the wife of King Lot; and he gives Modred a primary function, both in this poem and in *Lancelot*, in bringing on the catastrophe, and Lancelot only a secondary. Arthur is thus a tragic figure, whose fall is due to his own sin. Tennyson eliminates Arthur's paternity of Modred in order to make Arthur a symbol of perfection; Modred thus becomes a minor figure and Arthur a symbol of the perfect soul, static in himself, and destroyed gratuitously from without.

and look to his kingdom, and then departs. The king calls Dagonet and asks him to sing, but Dagonet says that he cannot, and the king dismisses him and meditates bitterly alone.

In the course of this conversation, both Merlin and Arthur remark that they will never see the Grail, each admitting himself unworthy of it. This differs from Tennyson's treatment of the matter, for Tennyson exhibits the quest for the Grail as an example of otherworldly asceticism and as one of the forces disrupting the kingdom; Tennyson's Arthur holds himself aloof from the quest because he disapproves of it. Robinson, however, depicts Arthur as a sinning mortal, who indicates perfection by his divergence from it instead of by his embodiment of it, and who is in a fair measure to blame for his own tragedy; Robinson thus relieves Arthur of the impossible burden of perfection assigned him by Tennyson and relieves Guinevere of the equally impossible burden of causing the downfall of a kingdom by setting the example of unchastity to a lot of battle-hardened soldiers. It is true that Tennyson had more or less clearly in mind his idea of an allegory of "Sense at war with Soul" in creating these and the other figures, but the allegory is seldom quite clear in his mind or in ours, and the poems live as narratives about people, and the people when not dull are too often incredible. Robinson knows that he is writing about people, although he is quite aware of the principles affecting their lives. Tennyson's Arthur achieves the ultimate in self righteousness in this connection, and goes quite beyond anything in his parting speech to Guinevere: he finds the Holy Vision beneath him. If one is to forgive him his speech to

Guinevere, one must see him in a purely allegorical capacity as perfection of soul, and even then there are difficulties; if one is to forgive him his rejection of the vision sent him directly by God, one must see him as a worldly monarch confronted with duties to a mixed world, and here there are likewise difficulties. But one cannot have him as both.

The king, after Merlin leaves him, thinks bitterly that Merlin cares more for Vivian than for himself and is anxious to return to her. The fourth section thereupon introduces a flashback of ten years, which gives us Merlin's life in Brittany with Vivian. Vivian is not presented as an enchantress, but rather as a beautiful, witty and self-centered woman, who falls in love with Merlin as he with her and insists that he leave the court for her sake. He goes to her castle of Broceliande and withdraws from the world; this is given as an explanation of the "living grave" of the legend. After about ten years Dagonet arrives as a messenger from Arthur, asking Merlin's help. Merlin goes to Camelot, accomplishes nothing, and returns to Vivian. Merlin's concern for Arthur's fate now comes between him and Vivian; he broods on Arthur as a great man undone by sin (the begetting of Modred) and by foolishness (the marriage to Guinevere and his preoccupation with the consequences, to the neglect of Modred's activities). Vivian is contemptuous of all ideas of sin, cannot understand, and is jealous; and Merlin finally leaves her again for Camelot.

The seventh and last section opens with Gawaine and Bedivere looking down over Camelot from Merlin's rock. They talk of the civil war already begun. Modred has killed Tor and Lamorak; Lancelot has carried off Guinevere and has killed Gawaine's brothers in doing so; Gawaine is bitter and violent, and Bedivere tries unsuccessfully to persuade him to try to persuade the king to make peace. Dagonet, who has joined them, summarizes the situation.

See *Merlin*, lines 31-33 on page
301 and lines 1-20 on page 302 of
Collected Poems of Robinson.

Gawaine and Bedivere leave, Dagonet speaks to himself, and Merlin appears. Merlin and Dagonet talk of the Grail and of how it removed knights or discouraged them by showing them their weakness. Merlin is old, as a result of his having entered Time, or normal human relations, to join Vivian, and his world is crumbling. He makes Dagonet promise not to mention their meeting, lest men should doubt his loyalty to Arthur: he is not going down to Camelot, because he knows that the end is destined and that he can alter nothing.

The poem shows something of Robinson's style at its worst and at its best. In *Merlin*, as in all the long poems, there is too much conversation, and Robinson shows a taste for a certain kind of conversation of which he is far from being a master—that is, for the playful and whimsical. This kind of conversation occurs most frequently, although not invariably, between men and women; at its best, it is not without a certain charm, but much of the time it displays a pedantic briskness or even pertness which is very hard to endure. One of the pleasanter specimens occurs at the beginning of the fifth section, where

67

Vivian's serving-man is preparing Merlin for his first banquet at Broceliande.

> See *Merlin*, lines 6-26 on page 268
> of *Collected Poems* of Robinson.

In certain lines from the sixth section, however, the style is at its worst; Vivian loses both her personal and her poetic dignity—she speaks like a school-girl and like the poetic creation of a school-girl.

> See *Merlin*, lines 13-16 on page
> 288 of *Collected Poems* of Robinson.

The greatest poetry in *Merlin*, and some of the greatest in Robinson, is to be found in the concluding pages.

> See *Merlin*, lines 31-33 on page
> 312, the entire page 313 and lines
> 1-7 on page 314 of *Collected
> Poems* of Robinson.

This appears to me to be great writing and well beyond anything in the *Idylls of the King*. The dry movement so familiar in Robinson's blank verse has vanished; the language is weighted and sinuous, yet is wholly without ornament.

The power is the final result, however, of the concept back of the poem, the concept of human tragedy as the consequence of a falling away from wisdom, and of the falling away as inevitable. The difference between Robinson's concept and Tennyson's, a difference more fully and powerfully developed in the *Lancelot,* may be seen in lines 14-16 on page 313 of *Collected Poems.* Robinson's Arthur is a mirror in which imperfect humanity may view itself; Tennyson endeavors to make of his Arthur a model for imperfect humanity to emulate. There are various difficulties inherent in Tennyson's attempt which are all but insuperable. Perfection, in its nature, is unchanging; it is desirable, and presumably we labor to come closer to it, and in that labor is the narrative of the spiritual life and its drama, and in the disastrous failure or frustration of the labor is tragedy. But perfection itself remains both unchanging and so far as the actual conditions of this life are concerned an abstract ideal. It may be a fit subject for the contemplative poem as it is for the contemplative life; but it does not lend itself to narrative. Arthur, Tennyson's embodiment of virtue, remains therefore a mere backdrop, in himself no more important than a statement of general principles would have been. And there is another even greater difficulty which Tennyson failed to see: to embody perfection in human form might be regarded as the prerogative solely of God. To define perfection as best one is able, and labor toward it as best one is able, is necessary and human; but to offer one's own human creation as the Divine Incarnation may seem blasphemous to some and will certainly seem ridiculous to many. To succeed in the effort, in any event, one must possess an all but superhuman wisdom. According to Christian doctrine, man fell with Adam and perfection has been realized only once since that event, in the person of Jesus, or of God become man. I speak in all humility as one of the unregenerate; I am not a Christian, and I look at these matters al-

69

legorically, for lack of a better method. But the Jesus of
the Gospels displays infinitely more both of the human and
of the divine than does the Arthur of the *Idylls*. Jesus, no
matter how one looks at him, is a Savior; the Tennysonian
Arthur, in spite of all one may do for him, is a Victorian.
Tennyson's morality did not surpass that of the sentimental
segment of the Victorian period of which he was a part;
it was neither a universal morality nor a respectable ap-
proximation of one, as one can see briefly by comparing
the story of the Magdalen to the story of Guinevere. Had
Tennyson's Arthur, like Robinson's, been jealous, he would
have been human; but he was above jealousy and set himself to judge. His judgment is guided by the literal principles of respectability; he takes no account of the suffering or change of the spirit. To call him a whited sepulchre
would indicate a failure to appreciate the delicate tinting
of Tennyson's style, but he is perhaps a kind of roseate
sepulchre. Robinson's Arthur, in spite of any peculiarities
of Robinson's mind and style, is human, as Robinson's morality is humane and intelligent; Robinson does not try to
embody perfection in a single mortal, but indicates the
real existence of wisdom by showing various lapses from
it and their results.

Such unity as *Merlin* attains, however, resides in the
character of Merlin and in the collapse of his two worlds.
He sees Arthur's kingdom collapse for reasons which he
had foreseen and which he believes to have been fated;
yet it is because of his love for Vivian that he is not present
to help Arthur when the disaster is approaching. Yet his
love for Vivian is not strong enough to force his love and
grief for Arthur from his mind, so that Vivian turns from

him in jealousy. His two great passions are therefore in conflict, and if we discount Merlin's view of Fate, each is in some measure to blame for the disaster befalling the other. Merlin's view of Fate, however, is central to the poem, and the possibilities of the alternative relationship are never fully explored. The unity of the *Lancelot* is of a very different kind; in the *Lancelot* the themes which are indicated in the frame of the *Merlin* are developed fully and dramatically, as are other themes of even greater importance.

3

Merlin appeared in 1917, the year after *The Man Against the Sky. Lancelot* appeared in 1920, the same year as *The Three Taverns. Avon's Harvest, Etc.* appeared in 1921 and *Dionysus in Doubt* in 1925. Most of Robinson's great poetry occurs in these collections, though some is earlier, and the fact might seem to support the theory of a later decline in his power. However, in the ten years remaining of his life, he wrote almost no short poems, and except for *Tristram*, with the plot and theme of which he tampered seriously, he invented the plots of his later long poems, with unfortunate results. The invented long poems, *Avon's Harvest* and *Roman Bartholow*, both of which fall in the great period, are no less remarkable in their failure than those which follow, and contain nothing as good as parts of *Amaranth*, the next to the last of Robinson's works. It seems to me obvious, as I shall later endeavor to show, that the difficulty lay not in the state of Robinson's talent but in his endeavor to apply it to forms which he understood insufficiently well.

Robinson opens his poem, as for the greater part he develops it, in his customary manner, a manner which is later to become a destructive vice and which even as early as *Merlin* and *Lancelot* does sufficient damage: he allows his reader to overhear a conversation. Lancelot and Gawaine are talking of Lancelot's intention to leave Camelot; Lancelot is sullen and is only formally friendly. Guinevere enters, and Gawaine takes his leave, and the second section is then devoted to a conversation between Lancelot and Guinevere. Guinevere says that Gawaine knows of their love and that they are really at his mercy. Lancelot replies that Gawaine is as friendly toward them as he is capable of being toward anyone, that it is not Gawaine whom he fears, but Modred, for Modred desires the queen, and he, Lancelot, is leaving the city. Lancelot appears to be haunted by the thought of the Grail. Both are restless and unhappy in their love, and both are aware of the doom impending over Camelot. Guinevere tells Lancelot that the king is leaving that night for Carleon or Carlisle to hunt, and asks Lancelot to come to her. The third section, a brief one, contains a monologue spoken by Lancelot, which summarizes the motivating situation of the poem.

See *Lancelot*, lines 31-32 on page 382, the entire page 383 and lines 1-18 on page 384 of *Collected Poems* of Robinson.

In this passage we see Lancelot on the point of doing that which both he and Guinevere do at the end, on the point of abandoning love in favor of a life of religious contemplation; yet the Queen at this stage has no such idea, and because of her invitation and the melancholy remnant of his passion for her, he postpones his departure to spend another night with her, and he meditates here on his weakness. The passage does not contain the greatest writing in the poem, but it nevertheless contains great writing, especially in the first half; and in the movement of the whole of it we get the feeling of the morose and massive man, unable to act for the moment from his conviction, and seeing himself for what he is in the interlude. It is this postponement of decision which precipitates the action of the poem, an action which brings Lancelot back in the end to his original intention and results in the conversion of the Queen.

In the fourth section we learn that the King's hunting trip was a trap; he pretends illness and returns that night to Camelot, taking Lancelot and Guinevere together. It is through a conversation between Gawaine and Bedivere that we begin to learn of the situation. Gawaine reproaches himself for having joked with Lancelot in the garden.

See *Lancelot*, lines 30-33 on page
387 and lines 1-10 on page 388 of
Collected Poems of Robinson.

Gawaine's description of himself and of the situation is acute. But what follows, though it is not bad in itself and contains a certain amount of necessary statement besides, is relatively diffuse and undistinguished. Had Robinson

73

been able to cut and condense his writing to this quality, or to a quality as good as that of the preceding passage which I have noted, the poem would stand as one of the great narrative poems of the European tradition. Bedivere reproves Gawaine for blaming-himself, and then the King enters, crushed by his discovery. The last three pages of the section are a disturbed monologue by the King, from which we learn that Lancelot has fought his way out of the court and killed twelve knights. The law requires that the Queen be burned, and the King believes that the execution is now taking place.

This long speech by the King is another indication of Robinson's weakness. By using this speech he endeavors, in the first place, to convey certain information for its own sake, information which, had it been conveyed directly, could have been conveyed with greater brevity and power, and, in the second place, to exhibit the King's collapse. In regard to the second matter, he is guilty of the fallacy of imitative form. It is reasonable that the King should collapse, but not that the style of the poem should do so; the King in a state of collapse cannot comment in distinguished poetry upon his own condition or upon anything else, and the poet should never abandon his distinction. Had the King been permitted enough presence of mind to comment briefly on his condition and the cause for it, and had the remainder of the substance been conveyed by Robinson directly or through another speaker, the passage could have been shorter, better organized, and finer in detail. As it stands, it wanders in imitation of a confused mind and like a confused mind says nothing effectively. The downright feebleness of the passage will be evident if these lines are compared to the passages to which I have already referred.

> See *Lancelot*, lines 28-34 on page
> 392 of *Collected Poems* of Robin-
> son.

These lines are the concluding lines of a section and a speech; moreover, they are spoken by a king, presumably by a great king. There is a kind of contemptible feebleness about them; one feels that if the King could have done no better, the poet should have done so. That the King should collapse is understandable, but the collapse should be understood in terms of his greatness. As it stands in this naked exhibition, it is not a fall from greatness but a negation of greatness.

In the fifth section the same scene continues, but is interrupted by the sound of battle and then by the entrance of Sir Lucan, who announces that Lancelot and a band of knights have carried off Guinevere and killed many unarmed knights in doing so, among them Gareth and Gaheris, Gawaine's favorite brothers. Lucan admits that it was Lancelot individually who killed these two in the tumult, though he says that Lancelot did it inadvertently. Gawaine is overcome with fury and hatred, and Arthur asks to be left alone with him. Arthur sees this as the beginning of the end. Sir Lucan, who has no other function in the poem than the one thus mentioned, is presented as a kind of Polonius, an elaborately and tediously formal and circumstantial talker, but he lacks the pathos of Polonius as well as the diluted dignity; and there is no excuse for

75

such characterization in the poem. If he is meant to be humorous, he is a failure; if he is not meant to be humorous, he is inexplicable. He infuriates his listeners against himself and leaves the reader bewildered by Robinson.

In the sixth section, we find that Gawaine has goaded Arthur to make war on Lancelot, and that Arthur has laid siege to Joyous Gard. Lancelot has the stronger party, but he refuses to employ it to end the war, although both Bors and Guinevere urge him to do so and to kill Arthur and Gawaine; they can see no other way out of a bad situation. Lancelot's answer to Guinevere is one of the finest passages in the poem, and gives a very impressive summary of Lancelot's character, the real motivating force of the poem, as it appears at this stage of the action.

See *Lancelot,* lines 5-35 on page
407 and lines 1-27 on page 408 of
Collected Poems of Robinson.

After the violent action of rescuing the Queen, Lancelot has returned to a state of mind resembling that in which he was at the beginning of the poem, except that it has been complicated by the development of the action. He is loyal to his desire for a new life, and he sees the Queen as that which binds him to the old; but he is loyal to the Queen and cannot leave her to vengeance or to chance; and his very loyalty to his new desire binds him both to defend her and to spare the King. She is able to understand nothing of this, a fact of which he is aware. Her moral and intellectual understanding has remained simple; his own

76

has been complicated by a perception of a fuller life than he had before suspected possible, a perception represented by the vision of the Grail.

The next day the Bishop of Rochester brings a letter demanding in the name of the Pope that Lancelot return the Queen to Arthur and with it Arthur's promise that she will be unharmed. Lancelot agrees, and the Queen faints at the news.

In the seventh section Lancelot and Guinevere talk of Lancelot's decision at great length. Guinevere pleads with him, but fails to move him. The speeches are too long and are none too effective, and toward the end Guinevere breaks down as Arthur had done when he thought she was in the fire, in a manner that is painful mainly because it is unsuccessful poetry. Nevertheless, the section is powerfully conceived, and in certain passages in which the motives of Lancelot are explained, either by Lancelot or by Robinson, the writing achieves a power similar to that in the best passages which I have noted. Lancelot is moved by various considerations. He feels that their love had been wrong and that they have been faced so obviously by the moral issue that they cannot go on without degrading their love; and at the same time he is haunted by thoughts of the Grail, that is, by thoughts of devotion to a higher life than he has before known, a devotion impossible while he is fastened to an illegitimate love.

See *Lancelot*, lines 20-30 on page 415 of *Collected Poems* of Robinson.

He has come to a point where a decision is necessary; that is, he has seen the issue which he had not seen previously, and which she has not yet seen. If he does not adhere to his present decision, he feels that he will degrade both their future and their past, whereas their past, if it is ended now, is not without its justification.

> See *Lancelot,* lines 28-33 on page
> 416 and lines 1-25 on page 417 of
> *Collected Poems* of Robinson.

This passage is excellent, though not as fine as some to which I have referred. I should perhaps interrupt the comment on the action, however, to mention two defects which occur in this passage, one of which occurs elsewhere in this poem and one of which occurs from time to time throughout Robinson. The recurring use of the terms *Vision* and *Light* to represent that for which Lancelot is turning from the world is very weak; the effect is that of a somewhat sentimental cliché, partly because the words themselves are stereotyped, partly because their use represents an evasion of exact statement. The analysis of Lancelot's state of mind as he hesitates between his two discrepant modes of life is rich and perceptive; the mode of life which he wishes to leave is fully indicated; but that which he wishes to find is marked only by a stereotype, and the effect is bad. The second defect occurs in the last phrase, *One of these days.* Robinson has a taste for the familiar colloquialism which is probably natural in a poet who is the product of a region with strongly marked folkways; one can find the same taste in Frost and in Hardy, for example.

But through some defect of sensibility Robinson is not the master of such colloquialisms; his ordinary style is formal, and the colloquialisms almost always appear flat and out of place. Hardy's colloquial lines, in their context, at least, are often very fine; but when Robinson does something comparable, as in this passage, or as at the end of "Rahel to Varnhagen," [2] we too often have an awkward lapse and no more.

I must return to the story, however. Guinevere understands nothing of what Lancelot says to her, but pleads to remain with him. She says that they can live together in hiding in France, that God cannot begrudge them what little is left of their love, and that he can turn to his vision when she is dead. She says further that the word of Rome is not the word of God—a Protestant suggestion that would be an anachronism if the poem had any real place in time that mattered. Lancelot answers that two persons such as themselves could hardly live long in concealment, and that although the word of Rome may not be the word of God, nevertheless it has weight, and would bring on a greater war than the present one, and the war would be unjustified.

> See *Lancelot*, lines 5-23 on page
> 421 of *Collected Poems* of Robin-
> son.

This is Lancelot's final argument, from which he will not be moved, though Guinevere protests in a speech which is much too long, and which has the effect merely of frantic

[2] See Chapter 7, "The Poems of Medium Length," page 137.

and repetitious talking and not of the poetic concentration to be found in the passages which I have quoted. Lancelot takes Guinevere back to Camelot; he is formally banished by the King and returns home. Gawaine thereupon persuades Arthur to resume the war. Arthur's judgment is here overcome by Gawaine's passion, and he fails to consider the imminent danger from Modred.

In the eighth section we learn that the King has attacked Lancelot but has been forced to withdraw to defend himself against Modred. Gawaine, who has been mortally wounded, sends word to Lancelot that he wishes to see him and end the quarrel. Lancelot goes; they are reconciled; Gawaine urges Lancelot to help the King and then dies. This section is not bad but is not impressive. Gawaine, who is dying from a wound in the head, is far too garrulous for good poetry or for verisimilitude, and he displays the kind of flippancy to which I have objected in *Merlin*. Dramatically, the flippancy is not in place; stylistically, it is persistent, mannered and tiresome.

In the last section, Lancelot raises an army to help Arthur, and goes to England, only to arrive too late. He learns of the last battle and of the death of Arthur and of Modred; he then sends his army back to France, and goes on alone to find Guinevere, and finds her a nun at Almesbury. He is overpowered by his old love for her; Arthur is dead; and he begs her to return with him to France. She, however, during the long time that she has spent in the Tower of London, under guard to protect her from Modred, and awaiting the outcome of the war, has thought of what Lancelot said to her at Joyous Gard, and has become convinced that Lancelot was right; she has made her decision and abides by it.

See *Lancelot*, lines 4-11 on page
442 of *Collected Poems* of Robinson.

Lancelot, confronted with more favorable conditions, wavers again between his two worlds; but Guinevere, having been converted from the one to the other, is as vigorous in her new conviction as she had been in the old. This passage exhibits the old Robinsonian theme of endurance, and a little later Guinevere enlarges upon it; it is through endurance that one achieves self-understanding and self-possession.

See *Lancelot*, lines 20-33 on page
445 of *Collected Poems* of Robinson.

Each, then, renounces the other to achieve self-possession, while retaining the past, and they take leave of each other.

See *Lancelot*, lines 17-32 on page
446 of *Collected Poems* of Robinson.

The remainder of the poem, which is brief, describes the country about Lancelot as he leaves, and then describes his state of mind. Lancelot reverts to the position in which

Guinevere has recently sustained him, and realizes finally that it is only through loss that one achieves self-possession, or, to put it in older terms, that one must renounce life to win life.

> See *Lancelot,* lines 7-13 on page
> 449 of *Collected Poems* of Robinson.

Lancelot is not free, because of the Light; that is, because he has acquired understanding which he before had lacked, and of understanding one cannot divest oneself. Having acquired understanding which conflicts with previous habits or desires, one can sacrifice the habits or desires and achieve growth through tragedy; or one can try to sacrifice the understanding by refusing to live in accordance with it and thus corrupt one's existence. The few concluding lines which follow these last are not equal to the best which the poem contains, but they are a dignified conclusion to a great poem.

In the construction of this poem, Robinson has avoided the weakness of *Merlin* and the weaknesses of Tennyson. The action is not double, as in *Merlin,* but single; yet the initial act which precipitates the catastrophe, Lancelot's going to Guinevere, does not in itself bear the whole burden of the catastrophe; for Modred is ready and waiting, and the passionate nature of Gawaine is set in motion by an accident of the evening. Arthur, moreover, bears a fair share of the responsibility for his own downfall. Modred, in Robinson as in Malory, is Arthur's illegitimate son, not as in Tennyson and more genteelly, his nephew; Arthur, in begetting Modred, has set his tragedy in motion, and in neglecting Modred to war on Lancelot, even after the return of the Queen, he incurs further responsibility. Lancelot and Guinevere thus have no more than a reasonable share of responsibility for the related tragedies.

In Tennyson, on the other hand, Arthur is the human soul, whose downfall is brought about mainly by Guinevere, who represents the heart, or emotion, inadequately controlled by conscience and thus moving toward sensual sin; the result of Guinevere's action is the corruption of the court (human nature, and if we push the allegory at this point, Arthur's nature).[3] Merlin, as corrupted intellect, and the quest for the Grail, as improper asceticism, play unimportant parts in the downfall: in Arthur's final speech to Guinevere the real responsibility is assigned to her. Now Tennyson's allegorism is for the most part implicit and is also confused, and unless one watches him closely one misses much of it. His people seem for the most part to be offered as real people, though not very vigorously drawn; and his assignment of this responsibility to Guinevere in her capacity as woman is ridiculous if one considers it in the abstract but is curiously repulsive when one meets it in the text, for the tone of the assignment is that of

[3] Conflicting with this interpretation, of course, is the role of Arthur as the perfect soul, the Christ-like model, who after the corruption of his court remains impeccable and judges Guinevere. This conflict, however, along with a good many other conflicts, is in the work and is not of my devising. For an excellent analysis of such matters, see *Handbook to Tennyson's Works*, by Morton Luce, London, George Bell and Sons, 1895. See also *Tennyson: His Art and Relation to Modern Life*, by Stopford A. Brooke, G. P. Putnam's Sons, New York and London, 1894.

83

Victorian sentimentalism at its worst, of the moral sentiment corrupted by a lack of moral principles while main-
taining the forms of a superficial but rigid respectability.
The morality resembles the style: it has retained something
of the surface of a great tradition and is minutely sensitive to small shocks while wholly unmoved by great, and
it exhibits moments which deserve a better context.

Tennyson, moreover, is inferior to Robinson in another
respect: he never draws his concept into a single related
action, as Robinson does in *Lancelot*. Each "Idyll" allego-
rizes a fragmentary aspect of the theme, and the group of
Idylls is a group of related fragments, with their only
unity in the allegorical theme, with no unity in action.
Since each fragment is a small part of the theme, it is too
often trivial in itself and is spun out thin into little details of which the only value is that of gratuitous decoration, as in "Gareth and Lynette," or it is compounded of
preposterous melodrama, as in "Merlin and Vivian." Instead of constructing an action, Tennyson constructs a
series of footnotes to Arthur's farewell speech, and tries to
expand them into stories.[4] But Robinson gives us the fall
of Arthur's kingdom in a single unified story; and moreover, he gives us this merely as incidental, though closely
related, to his main action, which deals with the effort of

[4] One might reply in rebuttal to these objections that the reader
should forget the allegory and merely read the stories and their
poetry, in the same manner in which the reader of the fifteenth
century read Malory. To this I can only say that Malory is a writer
whom most literate persons admire but few have read, that his
narrative is confused, tedious and childlike except in a few scattered and brief passages. He offers the raw material of literature,
but nothing more. If we take Tennyson merely as a narrator, he did

the individual to achieve growth out of error, salvation out of tragedy. Lancelot and Guinevere understood their own experiences, in spite of their normal human obtuseness and weakness, and they grow before our eyes; the growth is traced with a good deal of subtlety. Their choice of the conventual life is the outward sign of the later stages of their growth; it is not, as in Malory, a sign of exhaustion and perhaps a mere prelude to purgatory, nor is it, as in Tennyson, merely a pathetic manner of getting themselves off the stage. They have sacrificed the limited life to the greater, passion to wisdom, the personal to the general. The sacrifice is genuine tragedy; that which is purchased by the sacrifice is genuine gain. Robinson's plan has the power to generate and support poetry as great as he can write, whereas for Tennyson's best poetry one will have to turn elsewhere. Had Robinson been as brilliant in the writing of his poem as he was in the planning, it could easily have had the greatness of a Racinian tragedy; the poem seems to have fallen short of this achievement mainly through Robinson's inability to criticize himself clearly, through a failure to cut and revise where cutting and revision were needed. As it is, the *Lancelot* is one of the few deeply impressive narrative poems written in English in more than two hundred years.

---

little to Malory but excise, rearrange, alter in the interests of gentility, and prettify in details of style. He offers no new psychological insight into character as such, if indeed he offers as much as Malory. His contribution is his allegorizing and moralizing of the stories; his value as a poet, as regards the details of his style, is generated by that contribution; if that contribution is unsound he is merely a poet for children, and incidentally one whom most children dislike.

4

The theme of *Merlin* is fate; the subsidiary theme of *Lancelot* is the tragic theme that human acts have consequences and that imperfect humans act unwisely and arrive at disaster, and the primary theme is the triumph over tragedy through personal renunciation and understanding. It is these themes which give power to the characters and the actions. The original story of Tristram had such a theme, represented by the incident of the love-potion; the theme was the power of physical passion, and this was the only important theme of the story. Robinson suppressed the potion and the primitive theme; he made other damaging but less serious changes, mostly related to this one; and what he had left was a popular love story.

The story of Tristram and Isolt is much older than the story of Lancelot and Guinevere, which may have been built up in part by the medieval romancers to introduce into the Arthurian cycle a love story which should rival the Cornish one. The story as we have it in Gottfried von Strassbourg and the Anglo-Norman Thomas, who belong to a relatively sophisticated period, contains embedded in it incidents and other details of an extremely primitive sort, and one can find details of perhaps greater antiquity in certain other versions. While it is true that the ingenious anthropologist can trace much of the Arthurian material to undated antiquity, the amount of primitive matter which remains in the story of Tristram in a relatively unchanged condition is rather large. In one incident of Thomas, for example, Tristram sends messages to Isolt by cutting marks on chips and floating the chips down a stream which runs through Isolt's bed-chamber, a method of communication which presupposes, as Bédier [5] points out, that the royal palace was little more than a hut. On another occasion, King Mark, in an endeavor to trap the lovers, calls the Queen, Brangwaine, Tristram and the dwarf into his room, and the entire household are bled for the sake of their health. Mark then has the tapers put out, complaining that the light hurts his eyes, and has the dwarf scatter flour on the floor, unobserved by the others, and then with the dwarf leaves the room. Brangwaine discovers the flour in time and warns Tristram, but Tristram foolishly tries to leap from his bed to the Queen's and in doing so opens his wound and bleeds profusely. He leaps back to his own bed, but both beds are stained with blood. Mark, upon returning, finds no tracks in the flour, but notes the bloodstained beds, which strengthen his suspicions. The whole incident is far from courtly, and again it would seem to indicate that bedroom accommodations, to say nothing of bedroom behavior, were very primitive. In the Welsh Red Book we learn that "Drystan, son of Tallwch, watched the pigs of Marc, son of Meirchyom, while the swineherd went with a message to Essylt. Arthur, Marc, Kei, and Bedwyr came all four, but failed to carry off a single pig, by ruse, violence, or theft." Bédier, who calls attention to all of these examples, informs us further that the name "Marc" means horse, and that King Mark was described in the early documents as having a horse's ears hidden under his hair.

[5] Thomas, *Roman de Tristan,* ed. Joseph Bédier, Société des Anciens Textes Français, 1902, 1905.

These things, and a good many others like them, may seem of minor importance. Robinson does not try to transmute them; he drops them. But they indicate the strong current of primitive feeling which runs through the entire medieval romance and gives it force and identity. Robinson drops this primitive feeling also, a feeling which is symbolized by the potion, but he does not succeed in replacing it with anything adequate. The story seems less amenable to modernized treatment than the story of Lancelot and Guinevere, most of which has its origins in relatively modern and sophisticated times.

I do not know whether it is important to mention the case of Queen Morgan in this connection, for Robinson's poem would have been more successful had she not been employed in it, and she is not a part of the original material, but belongs to the story of Arthur. Robinson chose to introduce her, however; and in doing so he introduced one of the most ominously ancient figures from the Arthurian cycle and at the same time stripped her of all her power. In the early Authurian stories,[6] Morgan is a fairy, as her name, Morgain la Fée, would indicate; she is a sister of Arthur and bears him a son, perhaps being thus the original of Morgeuse, the wife of King Lot, who bears Modred to Arthur. She is a mortal enemy of Arthur, and is a shape-shifter and a figure of evil. Miss Paton traces her with a good deal of plausibility to the Morrigan, an Irish goddess of war and death associated with Cuchulain. Perhaps Robinson's Morgan would trouble no one unac-

[6] See *Studies in the Fairy Mythology of Arthurian Romance,* by Lucy Allen Paton, Ginn and Co., Boston.

quainted with this background and should not trouble the reader who is acquainted with it, but Robinson has dropped so much and supplied so little that his portrait is disappointing; further, the evil of his Morgan, frail and attenuated though it is, is curiously merciless and inhuman, as well as indecent, and it remains unexplained by anything he offers.

These details, a few of many which might be described, I have mentioned merely as indications of the difficulty involved in treating a story so archaic.

Tristram was published in 1927. In general, it follows the old prose romance and the version of Malory more closely than it does the greatly superior version of Gottfried von Strassbourg and Thomas; but it departs in many respects from its sources.[7] The scene of the first section is laid in Brittany. Isolt of Brittany talks with her father, King Howell, of Tristram, who has visited them and left. She admits that she loves Tristram, and King Howell is distressed by this admission, for he feels that Tristram regards her as a mere child. The scene of the second section is in Cornwall, on the night of King Mark's marriage to Isolt of Ireland. Tristram has withdrawn from the festivities to meditate on his own part in bringing about the marriage and on his love for Isolt. His friend and former teacher, Gouvernail, comes to him from Mark to urge him to join the feast, but he refuses. Queen Morgan then tries

[7] For the reader unfamiliar with the early material and who is interested in obtaining a quick summary of it, I recommend the article in the *Encyclopedia Britannica*. The scholarship in the field, though extremely interesting, is endless, and this is hardly the place to go into it, nor in all likelihood am I the person.

89

to persuade him, but fails. She is attracted to him and tries to arouse his interest in her, but she fails in this also, and she finally leaves.

In the third section, Isolt's attendant, Brangwaine, comes to Tristram, and she is followed at once by Isolt. They talk of their love, and Robinson works into their conversation an outline of the previous history: Tristram's killing of Morhaus, the kinsman of Isolt, Isolt's healing of his wound, and Tristram's second visit to Ireland to ask Isolt's hand in marriage for Mark. This conversation is typical of Robinson; it is long and diffuse. The conversation is finally broken by a cry from Brangwaine. The lovers spring apart, and Tristram seizes his cousin Andred in the shadows and hurls him over the parapet. In the fourth section Mark appears just in time to grasp the situation. Tristram accuses him of having sent Andred to spy; Mark denies this, and orders Tristram to leave Cornwall at once and for life. Mark indulges in a kind of laboriously inverted rhetoric which is especially characteristic of the long poems on non-Arthurian themes but which is impossibly bad wherever it occurs.

See *Tristram*, lines 22-26 on page 630 of *Collected Poems* of Robinson.

Tristram leaves the court, walks for a few days, sinks exhausted, becomes unconscious with a fever, and wakens to find himself tended by Gouvernail and a peasant. They take him in a cart to a castle, where he remains ill for some time; as he begins to recover, he discovers that he is in the castle of Morgan, with the queen herself as his attendant. Morgan succeeds in seducing him but not in getting his love; he finally leaves, and Morgan is contemptuous of his behavior. He decides to revisit Brittany.

The fifth and sixth sections deal with an interlude in Brittany. Tristram fights and defeats King Howell's enemy, Griffon, marries Isolt of Brittany, and spends about two years in the kingdom. Finally Gawaine arrives from Camelot as a messenger from Arthur, who wishes to make Tristram a knight of the Round Table. Gawaine flirts harmlessly with Isolt and promises her that Tristram will return; Gawaine's speech describing Isolt to herself, early in the sixth section, is one of the two or three best passages in the poem, although it is light and descriptive poetry, not comparable to the great passages in *Merlin* and in *Lancelot*. Isolt says that Mark will kill Tristram; Gawaine answers that Tristram will return wiser than he left, and he implies that Isolt of Brittany is more worthy than Isolt of Ireland. Tristram and Isolt converse at length, and then Tristram and Gawaine leave for Camelot.

In the seventh section, Tristram is at Joyous Gard, the guest of Lancelot, and he discovers Isolt of Ireland there also. Mark was temporarily imprisoned for having forged the Pope's name, and Guinevere had taken advantage of the situation to bring Isolt from Cornwall to Lancelot's castle. This section, which is central to the poem, is devoted to a long love scene, made up almost wholly of conversation. It is here, I think, that we find the crucial weakness of the work. On the one hand, Robinson has discarded the love-potion and its implication of an uncontrolled physical passion; and on the other hand, his characters

91

have none of the intellectual and moral complexity of his Lancelot and Guinevere; Tristram and Isolt have almost no personal or characterizing qualities except their love, and their love is at once curiously disembodied and de-intellectualized, so that little save sentiment is left. Robinson's perverse ingenuity in stating simple matters is frequently offered as the shell of intellectualism, but it is a form with no content, an empty mannerism of style. Pure sentiment may serve as the substance of poetry, but it does not lend itself to extended treatment, and it does not lend itself, without help from other elements, to the characterization and strength of motive necessary in a long narrative. The lines which are employed to express the physical passion of the two lovers, and there are a few of these, are trite and have the effect of afterthoughts.

> See *Tristram*, lines 1-2 on page 687 of *Collected Poems* of Robinson.

And the lines dealing with the sentiment are spun out interminably.

The eighth section continues and concludes the idyll, in much the same manner. After some weeks at Joyous Gard, Tristram goes out on horseback; when he returns, he learns that Mark, who has somehow obtained his liberty, has kidnapped Isolt, who had been walking on the beach, and carried her off in a ship. Later Tristram receives a mocking letter from Morgan, telling him that Isolt is back in Cornwall, where he may see her if he has the courage, and he decides to make the attempt. In the ninth section, we find Mark talking with Isolt. Robinson has characterized Mark as sensuous and somewhat violent, but at the same time not without humanity and real affection. Mark expresses regret for what he has done, and says that Tristram may come if he will, that he himself demands only that he shall not see Tristram. The portrait of Mark in this passage is the best piece of characterization in the poem, but it is brief and incidental. Brangwaine comes in to say that Tristram is waiting, and she and Mark leave before Tristram joins Isolt. There is another love scene, in which Isolt's speeches are filled with premonitions of death. Andred comes upon the two silently and stabs them to death, and they are found by Mark, Brangwaine and Gouvernail. Some of the best poetry of the work is to be found in the early conversation between Mark and Isolt, in this section, and in the speeches of Mark toward the end.

Robinson's use of Andred strikes me as unfortunate. In the metrical version of Thomas, Tristram dies in Brittany, where he has been wounded in battle after leaving Cornwall. His wound is so serious that only Isolt of Ireland can cure it; she is sent for, and it is arranged in advance that if she comes a white sail is to be raised as a message to those awaiting, and if she does not come, a black one. She comes, and the white sail is raised, but Isolt of Brittany, in a moment of jealousy, tells Tristram that the sail is black, and he dies. Swinburne, who follows this version, extracts a good deal of power from the incident, in spite of his florid emotionalism. In this version of the ending, we have Tristram's death brought about as a dramatic consequence of his own actions, and through the effect of those actions on one of the major characters. In the prose romance and in

Malory, Tristram is stabbed to death by Mark, in a situation similar to that in Robinson's poem; and here again we have the death brought about by a dramatic passion in one of the major characters. But Robinson employs Andred, who is of no importance in the poem and could easily be dropped, and makes of him a tool of Morgan, who could just as easily be dropped. Morgan, in her jealousy and anger, has aroused Andred's love for her in order to make Andred jealous of Tristram; this minor action causes the catastrophe, and Isolt of Brittany and Mark, the wronged wife and the wronged husband, remain as passive bystanders.

The tenth section opens with Mark watching the ship which is carrying Tristram's body to Brittany. The scene then changes to Brittany, and King Howell talks with his daughter and tries to comfort her. This passage, describing Isolt of Brittany in her grief, is perhaps the best thing in the poem, though it is little more than a gentle elegy as compared to many passages in the earlier poems.

To compare Robinson's poem to the medieval versions would be pointless; it lacks their moments of power and something of their charm, but although it is equally garrulous it is without their confusion and childishness. There are four other versions in the past hundred years which call for at least brief comparison, however: the versions of Tennyson, Arnold, Swinburne and Hardy. Tennyson's treatment of the story in "The Last Tournament" is brief and notoriously ineffective. It is merely one of several incidents used to illustrate the decay of the court under the influence of licentiousness; the story is given in skeletal form, the characters are badly drawn, and the moral is pointed by melodrama. Arnold, one of the great poets of the nineteenth century in some four or five short poems and in a few additional passages, is normally one of the worst poets in English; his style is a deadly tissue of clichés and other amateur poeticisms. And his style is at its worst in "Tristram and Iseult" and renders the poem a complete failure. Hardy's short play, *The Famous Tragedy of the Queen of Cornwall,* is effective dramatically and retains the primitive simplicity that one associates with the original story, but it is bare and schematized; it contains two very beautiful songs, one sung by Isolt and one by Tristram, which are the finest things inspired by the legend in English but which form a minute portion of the whole work. Swinburne's *Tristram of Lyonesse* is more nearly comparable to Robinson's poem than are the others, though it differs from it widely. Swinburne follows the version of Thomas, which is superior to the version which Robinson uses and alters; Swinburne is aware of the underlying theme of the poem, the power of physical passion, and he tries to make the most of it; and he does a good deal with the jealousy of Isolt of Brittany toward the close. But he is no more successful than Robinson in depicting character, in fact may be less successful, for he is not even interested in the problem; and physical passion in Swinburne degenerates line by line by way of metaphor and simile into the description of landscape. The physical beauty of Isolt and of Tristram is compared, item by item and at extraordinary length, to landscape material; in moments of emotion (which are interrupted by little save description) the emotions of the characters flow out over the landscape, and the description of the landscape is supposed

95

to convey the emotion. Much of this descriptive material is lovely in detail, but it is all of a kind, it never stops and it buries the poem. Swinburne's style is the lush and heavy style of his school and period, and the hard old romance is lost amid poetical formulae; and Swinburne's taste for the overflow line, with the grammatical unit stopping abruptly after the overflow, introduces an element of recurrent and eventually exasperating clumsiness into his versification. Swinburne's style, like Robinson's, is diffuse and decadent; but whereas Robinson's decadence is the decadence of a moral tradition, Swinburne's decadence is the decadence of a literary tradition which has all but forgotten that there ever was such a thing as a moral tradition, and all experience is submerged in a uniform chaos of the senses. Robinson, like Henry James at his most tenuous, is decadent because he talks tirelessly and in too great detail about little matters which seem to him serious; details which would be serious if they were parts of a serious whole but which have been deprived of their source of seriousness in ways which Robinson does not understand; the style continues to operate, or to try to operate, in the absence of a subject. In small sections, Swinburne's style may appear more impressive than Robinson's, but in the long run it is easier to put up with Robinson's style, and his good passages are better than Swinburne's best.

6. THE OTHER LONG POEMS

THE POEMS WHICH I SHALL DISCUSS IN THIS CHAPTER ARE THE
following: "Captain Craig" (1902), "Avon's Harvest"
(1921), *Roman Bartholow* (1923), *The Man Who Died
Twice* (1924), *Cavender's House* (1929), *The Glory of the
Nightingales* (1930), *Matthias at the Door* (1931), *Talifer*
(1933), *Amaranth* (1934) and *King Jasper* (1935). The
dates of these poems are of interest in two respects if in
no others: the rapidity of composition of the later poems
may have a relationship to their inferior quality; and the
nineteen years separating the first two poems on the list
no doubt help to explain the profound difference between
what was attempted in "Captain Craig" and what was attempted in the others.

"Captain Craig," in fact, is not a narrative in the same
sense as the other poems. It is a character sketch, of about
the same sort as "Ben Jonson Entertains a Man from Stratford," but of much greater length; or rather, it is a character
but of much greater length; or rather, it is a character
sketch with more or less philosophical commentaries along

the way. The poem is said to be based upon the character of Alfred Louis, but Captain Craig is somewhat more beguiling than Louis appears in any available account of him. The narrator and a group of his friends pick up Captain Craig, a learned and perverse old failure who is near death, and look after him till he dies. The narrator endures more of the captain's conversation than does any other character. The poem consists of early conversations with Captain Craig, the narrator's irritated analysis of his own attitude toward the captain and of his fear that he is being taken in, three letters from Captain Craig, his death and funeral, and the reading of his testament.

Craig is an Emersonian philosopher, and the poem could no doubt be quoted at length to illustrate Robinson's transcendentalist sympathies, but I cannot avoid feeling that it ought to be quoted with caution. Craig is described as a helpless failure, and although the narrator displays him in a friendly and sympathetic way, he likewise regards him ironically; I see no reason to believe that Craig is offered as a genuine embodiment of wisdom. The protagonist of "Mr. Flood's Party" is treated in much the same spirit, but one is hardly to understand from that treatment that the poet is recommending drunkenness; we are merely given the man, his pathos, and his courage, or what there is of his courage, amid his confusion. When Craig is picked up starving and is fed, he feels "No penitential shame for what had come . . ."

See "Captain Craig," lines 8-13 on page 115 of *Collected Poems* of Robinson.

THE OTHER LONG POEMS

This is what Emerson ought to have said had he ever been caught in the same predicament; the doctrine is orthodox, and there is much more like it in the poem; but it ought to be taken in its context. Craig, in one of his letters, for example, tells the story of Count Pretzel von Würzburger, the Obscene, a character said to be drawn from Joseph Lewis French. Craig says of Count Pretzel many of the same things that the narrator says of Craig, yet Pretzel is described as "a vagabond, a drunkard, and a sponge," and it seems unlikely that Robinson admired either Pretzel or French without certain qualifications, no matter how amusing he may have found them. In characterizing these men Robinson is depicting wasted and incomplete geniuses, and their opinions are the opinions of wasted and incomplete geniuses. The poem is a character study, not a didactic piece, and it seems to me the part of wisdom to take these characters in somewhat the same spirit as one takes Falstaff. If I seem to labor this point, it is merely because there has been a good deal of effort, most of it I think naive, to deduce elaborate philosophical views from Robinson of recent years, especially by writers in certain learned periodicals who seem to be engaged in the academic game of gathering "evidence" without much regard to what the evidence means. The poem has real pathos and is amusing for many details along the way, but like so many of Robinson's poems which are not restrained by rime, it is redundant and wears out its welcome. It treats its subject, however, with more balance than does *Amaranth*, written many years later, when the consideration of such characters appears almost to have become a morbid obsession.

99

"Avon's Harvest" is a poem dealing with a pathological relationship which may or may not be tinged with homosexuality. The narrator calls on Avon, who is ill, and who promises to tell his story. The two of them talk for some time, but with a subtlety so characteristically Robinsonian that no light is thrown on the subject of the poem for a great many lines. While they talk, Avon's wife walks restlessly in the next room. Finally we begin to get the story. When Avon was sixteen years old and living at a boarding school, a new boy came. Avon found this boy profoundly repulsive, but the boy attached himself to Avon with intense affection.

See "Avon's Harvest", lines 9-34
on page 522 and lines 1-23 on
page 523 of *Collected Poems* of
Robinson.

Avon hated the boy, yet felt remorse for his hatred and let the relationship continue. Finally the boy boasted to Avon of a lie he had told reflecting on the honor of another boy in the school; and Avon abused him and then hit him, knocking him down. The story became known, and the new boy left school the next day. He and Avon met as he was leaving, and he told Avon that he would know where Avon was until he died. Every year after that, on Avon's birthday, Avon received a post-card with the words: "I shall know where you are until you die."

They met later in Rome, and again in London; finally the man was listed as missing in the sinking of the *Titanic*, and no more cards came. The October before the conversation which forms the greater part of the poem, Avon had gone to the Maine woods with a friend. After two weeks his host paddled to the nearest town to shop, and spent the night there. At twilight, Avon, alone in the cabin, felt the gathering of horrible presences in the scene about him. He entered the cabin and built a fire, but his feeling remained unaltered. He lay down on a bunk in his clothes and fell into a kind of cataleptic sleep, from which he opened his eyes to see his enemy. The figure approached slowly, with an expression of intense hatred and sorrow, raised his hand, in which Avon saw a flash of metal, and struck. Avon lost consciousness and was found the next day by his friend. This was a year ago. He now tells the narrator that tomorrow is his birthday. The narrator leaves, but he is called back by Avon's wife a little before dawn. Avon is dead, and the doctor's words close the poem.

> See "Avon's Harvest", lines 11-21
> on page 573 of *Collected Poems*
> of Robinson.

The writing in this poem is nowhere better than in the first passage to which I have referred; in fact it is almost nowhere else as good. On the other hand it is seldom if ever worse than in the second passage; the style has the virtues of competent, if rather ordinary, prose. Both passages indicate a defect of Robinson's blank verse which becomes noticeable whenever the subject is not adequate to support great poetry: a mechanically repetitious beat, marked by heavily end-stopped lines. In the final passage, the end-stops are so heavy that the words *agree* and *child* when one

101

comes to them appear to mark the ends of grammatical units, in spite of the fact that *child*, if it did so mark an end, would result in nonsense; with the result that the phrases introducing the subsequent lines are left hanging and curiously weak. This comment may seem trivial; it is likely that the average reader does not notice such matters; but that the average reader is unaffected by them, I doubt—they are small flaws, and the total, even if vague, effect of a good many such flaws is a blunting of the style. There are many such flaws in the later narratives.

The story itself is a horror story, of the kind to be found in many popular prose collections; the story never gets beyond the intention to awaken horror for its own sake, in spite of the psychological subtleties suggested in the earlier parts, and it thus fails to lift the verse to poetry—it lacks the seriousness which alone could motivate a great poet to his best writing. As a study in remorse, it is inconceivable, for the consequences are out of all proportion to the initial act; as a study in fear, it is inconceivable for the same reasons; unless in both cases we assume that Avon is abnormal at the outset and progressively becomes insane. And if we assume this, we have abandoned the realm of normal human nature and of moral action. If the story is to be regarded as a serious study in abnormal psychology, there are two objections to be made to it: we do not know enough about the actual facts of the case to understand it, and abnormal psychology is a proper subject for science but not for poetry, as it simply lacks general relevance; we may understand the abnormal mind theoretically and we may pity it, but we cannot share its experience in any important amount. These are the reasons, I believe, why the writing is mediocre; the fact that the writing is mediocre seems to me indisputable.

Roman Bartholow, one of the longest of the poems, is one of several attempts to do a realistic novel in verse. In the first section, Bartholow is recovering from an illness, apparently a mental illness. His wife, Gabrielle, has not known how to help him, but his friend, Penn-Raven, has appeared accidentally, stayed, and cured him. The entire story of the malady, the care and the cure is brief and vague, and this is a serious defect, for Bartholow and his wife are the primary characters and we never understand either except in the cloudiest of terms; Penn-Raven alone acquires a certain clarity, and his function is secondary. Umfraville, a grotesquely formed but scholarly and intelligent neighbor, calls and talks to Bartholow and leaves a gift of trout. Umfraville apparently dislikes Penn-Raven, and he tells Bartholow to visit him if he should ever need help.

The second section opens with Bartholow and Gabrielle talking before breakfast. Bartholow is joyous at his recovery and is in love with Gabrielle, but Gabrielle is cold and evasive. Penn-Raven comes in, and Robinson gives a brief description of his appearance which is a clue to his character and behavior.

See *Roman Bartholow,* lines 27-33 on page 748 and lines 1-10 on page 749 of *Collected Poems* of Robinson.

103

We have in this passage an indication that Penn-Raven is intelligent in certain respects, that he is sensual and weak as well as sensitive, and that he dupes himself as effectively as others; he is the unscrupulous sentimentalist with friendly intentions who can find in all good faith the best of motives for whatever he may have done. Gabrielle refuses to eat the trout when she learns that Umfraville has brought them; Bartholow is upset, wonders about Umfraville's remarks of the day before, and leaves his own breakfast; and Penn-Raven, with some pleasure, eats all the trout and goes for a walk. Bartholow and Gabrielle continue to quarrel somewhat subtly about rebuilding their life together. Finally, as Penn-Raven is seen returning in the distance, Bartholow realizes that Penn-Raven is the cause of the trouble, although the poem barely hints at this realization.

In the third section, Bartholow goes down to the river to get some exercise by cutting down a tree. Penn-Raven sits above and watches him and presently is joined by Gabrielle. The two of them talk for a long time, although nothing really emerges from the conversation except that Gabrielle had had three years of unhappiness with Bartholow in his sickness, and one gathers that she had attached herself to Penn-Raven during that time. She is unhappy; we do not know why. And there is the bare hint that Penn-Raven wants to make his escape.

In the fourth section, Bartholow and Penn-Raven meet by the river. They engage in a conversation composed of innuendoes; neither knows quite what the other is getting at, and the reader is only a trifle better off. Bartholow walks away, while Penn-Raven returns to the house to make love to Gabrielle, who repulses him, saying that she is afraid they will be seen and that they were seen a week or so before by Umfraville. As they talk, it appears that Gabrielle had yielded to Penn-Raven when Bartholow seemed hopeless and when she was desperate, but that now she regrets it; Penn-Raven is bitter and scornful. In the fifth section, Gabrielle broods unhappily on the wreck of her life, and Bartholow returns to find her exhausted and despairing, with the story more or less on her face. As they talk, the facts come out, to some extent, and both realize that everything is over between them. It appears, though very subtly, that Gabrielle loves Bartholow again but sees the situation to be hopeless; she leaves the house, and walks down to the river.

In the sixth section, Penn-Raven returns and admits indirectly (nearly all of the admissions in these poems are indirect) that he knows that Bartholow knows everything. Bartholow curses him, leaps at him and, by virtue of the suddenness of the attack, knocks him down; but Penn-Raven is stronger and forces Bartholow into a chair. Bartholow orders Penn-Raven to leave, but they nevertheless go on talking, Penn-Raven in a somewhat sententiously sentimental way, the gist of his remarks being that the marriage could not have succeeded anyway and that its past failure was the cause of Bartholow's breakdown, so that Penn-Raven had done Bartholow a double favor in curing him and in breaking up his marriage. Penn-Raven talks in this vein for some time and with a great effect of perceiving his own virtue; Bartholow becomes more and more sickened and angry, and he finally gives Penn-Raven a check, which Penn-Raven accepts, to facilitate his going.

After Penn-Raven is paid and ordered out, there is a knocking at the door, and Gabrielle's body is carried in; she had drowned herself in the river.

The seventh section opens with a scene at the home of Umfraville. Bartholow knocks and is admitted; they talk of what has happened, and the comments of Umfraville, who is in a sense the official commentator, do not clarify the issues very greatly or rise to very great poetry.

> See *Roman Bartholow*, lines 23-
> 34 on page 835 and lines 1-25 on
> page 836 of *Collected Poems* of
> Robinson.

Bartholow then states his belief that Gabrielle had married him without loving him and had come to love him too late; his feelings about Penn-Raven remain mixed. In the eighth section Bartholow leaves his home forever, after giving Umfraville his books and talking over the entire affair with him.

This poem, like "Avon's Harvest", never rises above mediocre writing, and I believe again that the failure is to be explained by the material and by the method, which were simply incapable of generating important poetry. We know nothing of Bartholow except that he had been sick and was something of a reader; otherwise he is merely a man with a wife. We know nothing of Gabrielle, except that she was married to Bartholow and committed adultery with Penn-Raven during her husband's illness. Of Penn-Raven we know a little more, but we still do not know enough. For without some idea of the nature of Bartho-

106

low's illness and Penn-Raven's care of him, we have no clue to the kind of intelligence Penn-Raven is asserted to have—his intelligence is quite as hypothetical as Bartholow's illness. We do not know enough about any of the characters to know why Gabrielle succumbed to Penn-Raven and later came to love her husband; we neither know nor care. Yet in spite of the fact that we know very little about the people and the action, the poem is very long, and most of the length has been devoted to conversations among the people and about their affairs. Of these Robinsonian conversations I have already said a little and I shall have to say more; but I think it safe to assert here that they are essentially Jamesian, and in a bad sense: their purpose is to make the characters appear devious and subtle and therefore, presumably, interesting; to keep up the reader's interest by means of indirection; to convey the subtle inflections of feeling experienced by the characters through letting them talk, not of their subject, but around their subject. These people talk excessively of their feelings about subjects which are not explained or which are inadequately explained; I shall refer to a good example of this in my discussion of *Cavender's House*. The result is that we understand neither the characters nor the action, and hence do not understand the feelings which are the subject of conversation. The writing obscures the subject instead of clarifying it; the poem lacks substance and weight; and Robinson appears to endeavor to remedy this defect not by clarification but by redundancy.

In *The Man Who Died Twice* we have something of the pathological, but perhaps not too much; we have likewise Robinson's favorite theme, that of the man who is almost

107

but not quite an artist. Fernando Nash, the central figure, tells his story to the narrator. Nash had been a promising composer, and the narrator has found him, after having lost sight of him for years, beating a drum in a street revival meeting. Nash had years previously lost his friends because of his arrogance and their jealousy, and had ruined his talent through debauchery; he later became a convert to a Salvation Army type of religion and a street performer on its behalf; but he dies at the end of the poem as a result of new debaucheries. The poem is largely devoted to his account of certain of his ultimate hallucinations. An orchestra of rats plays a kind of symphony of the damned in the room in which he is dying. Later there is another and celestial symphony, in which he hears the music he might have made. His sense of his sin and his sense of his genius are equally great. He dies reconciled to his fate and to God, and leaves the narrator convinced that he was a great man. There is no obscurity in the narrative, and the story itself is almost impressive; it misses being impressive chiefly, I think, because Robinson seems to overestimate his character. One is not convinced that Nash is a great man, so that the story is more grotesque than moving. The rhetoric is forthright and more vigorous than that in most of the long poems, yet nowhere equals that of Robinson's best work; the trouble is partly that which I have just mentioned and partly the fact that the poem is too long and too talkative—Robinson too often seems to work on the principle that five mediocre lines are as effective as one good one.

Cavender's House is perhaps the most nearly perfect example of Robinson's worst vices as a narrator. It extends from page 961 to page 1007 of the *Collected Poems*. At the outset Cavender enters a house at midnight, his own house, which he had left years before and to which he has been compelled to return. "She" had called him, but she is not there. On pages 962 and 963 we find a characteristic example of Robinson's technique of ruminating on the unexplained.

> See *Cavender's House*, lines 28-33 on page 962 and lines 1-32 on page 963 of *Collected Poems* of Robinson.

Suddenly Cavender beholds her sitting in a chair, and she speaks at great length and bitterly on Cavender's nature and past behavior, though we are still uninformed of the facts to which she refers. This speech, interrupted occasionally by Cavender's own reflections to the same purpose, goes on for some pages, but without any clarification. On pages 970 and 971, for example, we have a passage, spoken by Cavender, as a part of this conversation about wholly unidentified events.

> See *Cavender's House*, lines 17-34 on page 970 and lines 1-21 on page 971 of *Collected Poems* of Robinson.

By this time we are conscious that "she" is some kind of hallucination, although on page 972 we suspect her of being a ghost; and in the line following the last passage we

109

learn that her full name is Laramie Cavender, that she presumably is or represents Cavender's wife. We learn that somehow Cavender has treated Laramie cruelly. They continue to talk, and bitterly, he because of her beauty and some suspected perversity of her nature, she because of his simple-minded possessiveness and imperception. On page 987 we learn (or think we do) that he has suspected Laramie of infidelity, and by page 990 this is fairly certain; on page 989 occurs the first suspicion that he has murdered her. On page 990 he asks her if she was actually unfaithful, and she answers that she does not know.

On page 994 Cavender notes that Laramie is not wholly Laramie, but seems to contain something of himself; she can read his thoughts, for example, and answer them without his speaking. She insists on their going down to an old cliff where they had often sat in the past. On page 999 we learn definitely that Cavender had killed Laramie, and apparently by throwing her over the cliff—this latter fact becomes certain on the next page. He pleads again that she tell him whether she was unfaithful. She ridicules him bitterly and seems too impersonal and cruel to be Laramie. She says she is not Laramie, but was created by Cavender himself. He is finally left alone and decides to confess his crime, which he had committed years before.

The poem is thus a study in conscience; but it is not until we have got to about page 990—not, that is, till we have read about thirty pages and are about seventeen pages from the end—that we know enough about the action to understand the poem as it progresses; and when we have arrived at that point, the portion which we have read is not remembered as a clear sustaining structure, but is remembered as a confused emotional haze from which we have at last managed to disentangle a few simple but necessary facts. The greater part of the poem is devoted to discussing the emotions arising from a very particular situation, but from a situation to which we are given no clues until three fifths of the discussion is past; to understand the greater part of the poem, we must reread it after we have once read to the end. A poet has a right to expect us to read his work twice or even many times, but not, I think, for this reason; the poem is defective in structure, for the rhetoric of emotion is unsupported either by narrative or by expository structure and the emotion remains necessarily as indefinite as everything else. When we have mastered the poem, we have no understanding either of Cavender or of Laramie. We have a man, in the abstract, who has murdered his wife, in the abstract, because he suspected her of infidelity, in the abstract, and who repents. The poem is merely a shell.

In *The Glory of the Nightingales* we have a story with a little more body, though not enough; and we have again Robinson's elaborate technique of withholding the story that he is telling, though not in quite so grotesque a form. At the beginning of the poem, Malory, a physician, is on his way to a place called Sharon, to murder Nightingale, who has injured him. Malory stops at the grave of Agatha on the way. He has loved her, and she is somehow involved in the wrong. He meditates on his past and present at great length, but we learn little about it. Malory imagines Agatha present as in life, and he talks to her; and we learn that Nightingale had in some way caused Agatha's death. He

111

passes the grave of Absalom Spinner, frowns, and meditates; one guesses that Spinner may have been Agatha's husband, to whom she was untrue, but the guess is a faint one. He takes a last look at the house that had once been his own and Agatha's and then proceeds on his way to Nightingale. After much walking and more meditation which throws no light on the facts, Malory comes to Nightingale's house, a palatial affair by the sea, and Nightingale welcomes him.

Nightingale is a helpless invalid, near death. Malory is surprised at this, and he hesitates, looking at Nightingale, who states his belief that Malory has come to kill him. Malory admits it. He turns away for a moment, and when he looks back, Nightingale has a gun pointed at him and disarms him. Malory, in handing over his own gun, says that Nature or God has beaten him to his revenge anyway. Nightingale remarks that he took his first pistol away from Absalom Spinner, who had come to kill him before his illness had set in; it seems that Nightingale had seduced Absalom's wife, who now turns out not to have been Agatha after all. After Nightingale had disarmed Absalom, he had given Absalom an annuity; Absalom had remained drunk on it for three years and then died. Malory, who has now abandoned his plans for murder, is too tired to leave, and is put up for the night.

The next morning Nightingale begs Malory to stay for one more day. Nightingale confesses that he had robbed Malory of money, and offers to repay it. They talk of Agatha; Nightingale had apparently robbed Malory of her also and then in some way destroyed her. It appears likewise that at an earlier time Nightingale had been in some large measure responsible for Malory's success as a scientist, apparently by advice and encouragement, and we discover that Nightingale has been a kind of wealthy patron to the town. He had been originally an honest and happy man and had almost won Agatha; then Malory had won her; Nightingale had become embittered and the rest had followed. Nightingale had laid and executed some plan to ruin Malory and Agatha, and had let the plan work. It now appears that Nightingale did not steal Agatha, but in some way had wrecked her life and killed her, apparently by a financial trick, Agatha having been too frail to stand the shock.

Nightingale now calls in a lawyer and wills his entire estate to found a hospital, it being stipulated that Malory shall be at the head of it. Then, when he is left alone, he shoots himself with Malory's pistol. Malory finds himself bound by the gift to serve mankind.

The poem, like *Roman Bartholow,* deals with the theme of the ambivalent benefactor, the hero of each poem being in the predicament of being greatly indebted to a scoundrel who has wrecked his life and about whom he cannot wholly make up his mind. This moral ambiguity is familiar in New England literature: one meets it for example in *Pierre* and in *The Confidence Man,* both by Melville, in *The Marble Faun* by Hawthorne, in *The Spoils of Poynton* and in many other stories by James. In Melville and James, however, and I think this is true of Hawthorne as well, in spite of the sentimental affectation of his style, the ambiguity is the result of a deep uncertainty, essentially metaphysical in its nature, which causes the writer a genuine anguish; in Robinson the quality of the feeling has

113

deteriorated, and we have a large admixture of the same exaggerated ingenuity which went into some of the more perverse short poems, such as "The Whip."

The manner in which the facts of the story are withheld weakens both action and style, and obscures the characters. This device often occurs in the novels of James, but ordinarily with a difference: in *The Ambassadors*, for example, the situation between Chad and Madame de Vionnet is fully developed, although as yet undisclosed, when the book opens, and the progress of the book is the progress of its disclosure; but the disclosure is not made directly to the reader—it is made, rather, to Lambert Strether, the chief character in the book, and the progress of the disclosure provides the experience which causes Strether's personal drama and his spiritual growth. In Robinson's poem, however, there is only one story, and it is really told backward: we start at the end, with the characters as nearly as possible in a state of mind appropriate to the end, a state of mind which hangs over the poem like a vague and unchanging cloud, and little by little we piece the story out till we get to the beginning. We do not see the development of a story; we read for sixty-two pages in a state of uncertainty as to what the story is; and when we get to the end we have nothing but a handful of bare facts, a few of them uncertain, for the form of the poem has precluded the possibility of the development of character or action and of the relation of motive to emotion. As in *Cavender's House,* Robinson tries to give us the emotion first and tosses the explanation in casually toward the end.

Matthias at the Door is a narrative displaying much the

114

same technique as I have been describing, but in this poem Robinson endeavors to impose a little mysterious and unsatisfactory symbolism on what should have been a realistic story. The time and place of the story are uncertain, likewise the social, economic and general setting of the characters; this uncertainty would not matter, perhaps, if the story were not so told that one keeps wondering about it. As the poem opens, Matthias is at home, or rather is exploring his property, near his house, at night. He lives in a rocky and wooded gorge. Garth, an old friend, appears and asks hospitality, and as the two converse one becomes aware of the self-satisfaction and self-righteousness of Matthias. They approach certain rocks that resemble some kind of ancient tomb, and Matthias warns Garth that this is a good place to stay away from, for it is so gloomy as to be dangerous. This particular place symbolizes the doorway to death, and it is the center of the poem, but why a group of curiously formed rocks in New England (if that is where we are) should exert the influence exerted by these rocks we never know. This is the center of the poem, as I have said, and it is pure fraud. Garth, it seems, knows the place well and points out an opening like a door, and suggests that they go down and admire it; he says that he himself will some day go there and knock. They go down, Matthias somewhat perturbed. Garth comments ironically on Matthias's character and on his present state of mind; it is impossible to grasp why Matthias is so upset by this adventure, for thus far we have been dealing merely with curious-looking rocks and not with an explicit symbol. Presently Matthias returns to his house and is welcomed by his wife, Natalie.

115

In the next scene, we have a conversation between Matthias and Natalie, from which we learn that Garth's body has been found within the "tomb." He had entered the place and then poisoned himself; he had been some kind of failure, but we never learn what kind. A new character, Timberlake, suddenly appears, and they all discuss Garth, at least ostensibly; indirectly but more seriously they discuss Matthias and his self-righteousness, and the attitude of Timberlake and Natalie toward him is a sceptical one. The tone of the conversation is very tense. Timberlake leaves, and Matthias and Natalie make up in some measure.

Natalie now thinks over what has occurred. We learn that she had formerly been almost in love with Garth but had found him too weak; she had been more nearly in love with Timberlake, but Timberlake was unreliable and would probably have been unfaithful; she had married Matthias mainly for practical reasons. Drawn by an irrational feeling, she goes down to the rocks, where she finds Timberlake. They talk of Garth with affection and of Matthias with affection qualified by irony. Natalie suddenly throws herself into Timberlake's arms and confesses that she loves him; they talk over their unhappiness and then go back. The next evening Matthias tells Natalie that he too had been there and had overheard them; Natalie tells him that she has always loved Timberlake, and Matthias goes away abjectly unhappy. Later, Natalie tells him that she has been false in thought only, and that they should try to be friends and continue. Matthias assents, but with no conviction, and they are coldly civil for a long time, Matthias loving Natalie but feeling injured, Natalie not loving Matthias but feeling sorry for him. Little by little Matthias deteriorates, as a result of frustrated passion; one evening, while drunk, he tries to kiss her, and she leaps away, denounces him, and strikes him. Matthias drinks himself to sleep, and next morning he awakes to find a note from Natalie: "Matthias, I am sorry. Natalie." He fails to find her in her room, and later he finds her dead by the door in the rock. We learn in this section that Timberlake, by debauchery, had deliberately made himself unworthy of Natalie because Matthias had once saved his life.

While Matthias is meditating on his loneliness, Timberlake appears and is welcomed. Timberlake is in very bad condition; he drinks too much and has a bad cough. Matthias exacts a promise from him that he will not kill himself, and then goes off on business. A heavy rain sets in, and Timberlake starts down to the door in the rock, and he is found later half way down and half dead, but he lives for some days, and during this time he and Matthias talk of their respective failures. Matthias then dreams that he meets Natalie in heaven, that she gives herself to him, and that she then shrivels to something abominable and he finds himself in hell, where she is a demon. He thinks of his loneliness and is haunted by thoughts of the door. An inner voice warns him away; the voice then seems to be the voice of Garth and it tells him that he cannot die until he is born. Then the voice seems to be that of Timberlake. He asks the voice whose it is, and the answer is Emersonian.

See *Matthias at the Door*, lines
29-30 on page 1149 and line 1 on
page 1150 of *Collected Poems* of
Robinson.[1]

For the rest, the gist of the conversation is simply this: that one must be born—that is, achieve spiritual life—before one has the right to die; but the nature of the spiritual life is not suggested.

The door in the rock symbolizes the door to death throughout the poem; but at the end it becomes the door to a new life (on this side of the grave) for Matthias. The transition is merely a play upon words; there is no organic relation of the two ideas. Nor is there any justification on the realistic level for the door to serve its allegorical function; nor is there any justification on the realistic level for it to exert the extraordinary attraction which it exerts for the characters. It is not, so far as one can discern, a real tomb or ruin; it is apparently an accidental rock formation in New England. To expect people in real life to be drawn as in this poem to commit suicide in such a place is ridiculous: certain locations, such as high bridges, appear, it is true, to attract suicides; but the attraction seems to be practical in its essence, and not symbolic. Robinson is forced to impose this improbable action on his characters, on the realistic level, in order to obtain an allegory which will

[1] At the risk of becoming tedious, I should like to call attention to the stylistic blunder in line 1, page 1150. *To us* is redundant; its redundancy is emphasized by its position at the beginning of a line in which it has no function and after the end of the line to which it belongs and in which it is unnecessary. This type of bad overflow is common in Robinson's least inspired blank verse.

lift his realistic narrative into the general and symbolic; but the two elements conflict rather than support each other, and the poem is ruined. The narrative, regarded strictly as realism, suffers from about the same defects that we have seen in *The Glory of the Nightingales* and in *Roman Bartholow*. The false symbolism seems to have been an abortive effort to get beyond these limitations. Robinson said to Nancy Evans,[2] "If you want to find out about my 'Transcendentalism,' read *The Man Against the Sky* and *Matthias at the Door*—it's in those poems." And Nancy Evans adds of the quotation marks around the word "Transcendentalism": "The quotes were in his voice." The Transcendentalism, in so far as it may be there, is stated briefly and vaguely; and its introduction into the second poem represents an error in method.

Talifer hardly deserves a summary. It is extremely long, not very complex, and unbelievably dull. Of all these poems, it is the only attempt at comedy in a pure form. It deals with Talifer, a noble and fatuous soul, Dr. Quick, a more realistic and less fatuous soul, Althea, a pleasant though mediocre woman, and Karen, an impossibly vain and learned lady. Talifer, who should be in love with Althea, is foolish enough to marry Karen; the marriage breaks up, and he comes back to Althea. Quick, who knows what Karen is, nevertheless is so foolish as to marry her next; he ultimately leaves her among the learned dons in England, and comes home to admire Talifer's family. The poem makes no attempt to be anything other than realistic, but the characterization is mediocre and the style is redundant.

[2] Nancy Evans, in *The Bookman*, November, 1932.

119

Amaranth cannot be considered a successful poem for more than one reason; but it contains more interesting writing than any other poem discussed in this chapter. It is a kind of nightmare-epic of failure, and it is the culmination of Robinson's life-long fascination with the near-genius. Fargo, a painter, realizes at the age of thirty-five that he has failed, and he destroys all his paintings save one, which, however, he knows to be mediocre. He falls asleep and dreams.

He dreams that he is on the wharves, where he was once tempted to drown himself but was stopped by a voice that told him to give up his art for another life. He is tempted again in his dream. He hears steps, and the voice speaks again, and he looks up to see a man, who reproves him for coming back to the "wrong world" and says he will take Fargo to see others who have made the same mistake. His name is Amaranth—"the flower that never fades," and as the poem develops, it is apparent that Amaranth represents Truth. Amaranth takes Fargo to the Tavern of the Vanquished. Fargo is called to a table, where Evensong warns him against Amaranth and introduces him to the rest of the company, all of them people who have chosen the wrong profession and made wrecks of their lives. Of these guests all have looked Amaranth in the eye and know themselves failures except Pink, the poet, and Atlas, the painter. Pink is quarrelsome and arrogant, and he finally demands that he be permitted to look into Amaranth's eyes. He looks, and he then goes out and hangs himself.

The dream changes, and Fargo is alone in a dark street; he hears steps, and obscene voices which ridicule him.

Suddenly he is surrounded by a crowd of foul men, the grave-diggers, with picks and shovels and with clay on their feet, who surround him and start to drag him off, but who are interrupted by Amaranth, who rescues him and disperses the crowd. These men doubtless represent the generality of critics and reviewers, who are incapable of perception or of judgment, but who live in the manner of scavengers by destroying or trying to destroy whatever they encounter; and they doubtless have a function in what is sometimes called the economy of nature in that they eliminate whatever is too weak or too moribund to withstand them. Amaranth takes Fargo to a rooming house; they enter a room, where the group from the tavern are looking at Pink, who is hanging dead. Evensong plays an elegy, and, as always when he performs his music, he apologizes, admitting that it is worth very little. Pink opens his eyes and insults them all, in one of the best passages of the poem.

> See *Amaranth,* lines 30-33 on page 1333, the entire pages 1334 and 1335 and lines 1-28 on page 1336 of *Collected Poems* of Robinson.

A bad poet, it appears, dies slowly.

Fargo finds himself in the streets again, with Amaranth. They enter another house and then proceed to the room of a woman, Elaine Amelia Watchman, and find Evensong with her, holding her hands; and with her also is Ampersand, her cat, who has the gift not only of talking

but of talking somewhat unpleasantly. Evensong under-
takes the introductions.

> See *Amaranth,* lines 12-13 on
> page 1339 of *Collected Poems* of
> Robinson.

Evensong wishes that the lady did not write, for he loves
her and her writing stands between them, but she finds
her life in her work. As they are about to leave, she suddenly decides to look Amaranth in the eyes. The whole
crowd, who now seem to be here, try to dissuade her, but
she looks and staggers back to the table. Evensong tries to
comfort her; he tries to read to her from one of her own
books, but the pages are dust. She screams and turns to
dust on the floor; Evensong carefully gathers the dust into
a small envelope and walks off to mourn, followed by
Ampersand.

These are probably the best incidents and contain the
best writing; there are several more incidents of considerable length and of the same purport, which it seems to
me might better have been omitted or greatly reduced.
At the end, Amaranth comments on everyone, bids farewell to Fargo, who is now free because he has faced the
truth wholly, and disappears. Fargo awakens to under-
take a career for which he is fitted.

It is not hard to understand why the subject of this poem
grew upon Robinson till he felt impelled to treat it with
something like epic pretensions. He was a very great man,
and one of the few great men of his period. He suffered, as
every such man suffers, from the difficulty that nearly all

of his contemporaries were not great and were likewise not very perceptive; consequently his greatness passed for something very different from greatness during the larger portion of his life. In his home village in Maine, in early life, he had been the local failure; in middle life, when his powers were at their greatest, he was praised at times, but grudgingly and often stupidly, and his work was overshadowed in the matter of public reputation by the work of one second-rate poet after another; it was not until the publication of *Tristram*, eight years before his death, that he achieved the reputation which he deserved, and when he achieved that reputation it was not for the work which deserved it. Throughout his life, or at least until the publication of *Tristram*, he had lived in genuine poverty, often on the charity of friends, and even in the last years he was scarcely wealthy. The conditions of his life threw him normally into contact with the intellectual failures, the debris of ambition; and there appear to have been periods when he wondered if he was not one of the same kind, although these periods must have been brief.

It was natural that he should have become obsessed with the subject; but the treatment in the poem is that of obsession, not of balanced judgment. The characters are almost as pathological as Avon and his enemy, and Robinson regards them with an intense seriousness which they do not really merit. They merit pity and understanding, and there is a good deal of both in the poem, tempered with a very humane irony; but they do not embody a central problem of the spiritual life, and Robinson appears to try to exhibit them as if they did. If one reads the poem for the sake of such passages as those I have quoted, it is the most rewarding of the long poems on non-Arthurian subjects, "Captain Craig" perhaps excepted, but it is not a successful poem, and the best poetry is not great. Much of the charm of the best passages results, I suspect, from the contrast between the grotesque nightmare of the action and the pedantic dryness of the rhetoric. Like all the other long poems, *Amaranth* exhibits the great Robinsonian vice of uncontrolled loquacity.

King Jasper is a poem of which the externals are realistic, but which is nevertheless more purely allegorical than any of the other long poems. It is primarily a social allegory; the ultimate difficulty is that the allegorical import is not entirely clear. Jasper is an industrial monarch; his wife, Honoria, whose name is an indication of a somewhat vague allegorical function, is haunted by ghostly hands working against Jasper and herself. Jasper, however, feels "living and invincible hands" working against him. Jasper's son, young Jasper, introduces Zoë to his parents; Zoë, he says, sees all through them.

See *King Jasper*, lines 14-19 on page 1408 of *Collected Poems* of Robinson.

Of Zoë, Robinson said in conversation: "Zoë isn't intended to symbolize life; Zoë is knowledge, and the child of King Jasper, who is ignorance. . . . Without ignorance there can be no knowledge." [3] Miss Kaplan comments on this passage with what seems to me excellent judgment: "Despite this authoritative interpretation, it is important to re-

[3] Hagedorn, p. 370.

124

member Robinson's customary irony and to reflect that in the poem the 'free' intelligence of Zoë is coupled with the younger generation's inability to understand the fears of their elders, with a total disregard of conscience, and responsibility, and in general with the kind of 'emancipation' which springs more from vitality than from reason, more from intelligent unconcern than from reflective experience." [4] It strikes me that more of Robinson's transcendentalist tendency, such as it may be, is shown in this poem than in most of the other poems in which it has been found; that Zoë represents vitality mistaken for intelligence in a traditionally Emersonian manner.

Young Jasper tells his parents that he and Zoë are married "under the stars and under God." Honoria leaves in indignation, refusing to speak to them. Jasper the elder says that he is afraid of Zoë, and asks if he is still going to school, and Jasper the younger replies that he can see pupils older than his father going to school to Zoë. In this part of the poem we have the first reference to the elder Jasper's friendship for old Hebron, and to his debt to Hebron, and to young Hebron's enmity for both Jaspers. King Jasper has a dream of old Hebron as the Old Man of the Sea, a dream which represents his debt to old Hebron and his inability to forget it. Jasper tries in the dream to escape to Zoë, and in his effort he falls into a chasm, the fall awakening him. Jasper receives an ominous visit from young Hebron, and little by little he becomes aware of the impending ruin, of the hands working against him. Young Jasper urges his father to take Honoria and leave, so that

[4] Estelle Kaplan, *Philosophy in the Poetry of Edwin Arlington Robinson*, Columbia University Press, 1940, p. 141, note.

125

he and Zoë may deal with the situation. King Jasper tries to send Honoria away, but she refuses; later he finds that she has killed herself. Somewhat later the insurgents of young Hebron's party set fire to the city, and the revolution is loose. King Jasper dies; young Jasper is killed by a shot; young Hebron enters, boasting of his success, and tries to seize Zoë. Hebron tells Zoë that the house is mined; she stabs him and escapes just in time.

The theme of the poem is something as follows. King Jasper, the modern industrialist, has erected wealth, power and civilization (civilization is represented by the charming but ineffectual young Jasper) on treachery to Hebron, who represents the common man. Honoria loves King Jasper for what he has accomplished and for his love for her, but at the crisis of the poem she is forced to abandon him and kill herself; Honoria, in so far as she represents honor, seems to represent it in a limited and conventional sense, except in her final act—throughout, for example, she is in jealous conflict with Zoë. Young Hebron, who comes in the role of the avenger, is represented throughout as a hard, grasping and imperceptive barbarian; he destroys civilization in avenging the wrong on which it was founded. Zoë alone survives; she alone understands and cannot be wholly possessed by anyone. As a social allegory, however, the poem is defective with relation to Zoë. Capitalistic democracy, as represented by King Jasper, fails; the revolutionary democracy, as represented by young Hebron, contains no elements of potential success— it appears to be the end of civilization. Now Zoë, as the allegorical representative of intelligence, no matter what kind of intelligence, cannot exist in a vacuum; she has to be possessed by someone, even though imperfectly, yet the only forms of social activity shown in the poem are incapable of possessing her. Either Zoë should have been destroyed or there should have been a solution. To tell us that there is no hope for civilization and then to say at the end, "Nothing alive/ Was left . . . There was only Zoë— alone"—this is merely balderdash; it is the final substitution of irresponsible sentimentality for thought.

See *King Jasper,* lines 20-22 on page 1488 of *Collected Poems* of Robinson.

It is fair to remember that this poem was composed during Robinson's final illness and was finished on his deathbed; yet the thinking is similar to that in certain portions of his earlier work.

If the poem is considered with reference to its plot, it is better in some ways than some of the earlier poems; it does not suffer greatly from the technique of withheld information, for one thing. But the characterization is so weak that neither plot nor allegory lives; and some of the allegorical devices, the ghostly hands, for example, which are repeatedly forced upon us, are so trite and so melodramatic that they make the depiction of real character and action next to impossible; character and action are betrayed by whimsy. The style is the wholly dead style of the later work, which is relieved in the last seven or eight years only in a few passages of *Amaranth.*

There are certain defects, then, which run through all or most of the long poems. There is the technical device of

127

withholding information about the subject under discussion, so that one never understands the nature of the (presumably) important emotions which are (apparently) being analyzed. Usually some of the necessary information is given us before we get to the end of the poem and after much of the analysis of emotion is long past; but frequently we get far from enough information even then, with the result that we feel Robinson is to be merely indulging a formulary ingenuity of style with nothing in particular in his own mind. Related to this device is the weakness of characterization; resulting in part from it, is the irresponsible redundancy of style.

I have pointed out earlier that Robinson appears in some of his shorter poems to have been influenced by Browning; the effect of redundancy and supersubtlety may have something in it from Browning, but in the main I think it comes rather from certain New England habits of mind. The redundancy and difficulty of much of Browning are due simply to a kind of systematic irrelevance, or progression by suggestion, to which we have become accustomed in such writers as Pound and Eliot: Browning lets his characters speak under the influence of excitement, and one thing suggests another, and they wander widely from the topic, return to it briefly, wander at length, return, and so on. The difficulty in Robinson is due rather to a kind of hallucinated sense of relevance, the product of the New England habit of moral introspection insufficiently guided by principle, and which may be seen plainly in certain of the works of Henry James. If one wishes to discern the difference between Browning and Robinson in this respect, one might compare the passages which I have cited from

128

Cavender's House with this passage, which begins with line 344 of the first part of *The Ring and the Book*:

> So said, so done—
> Rather so writ, for the old Pope bade this,
> I find, with his particular chirograph,
> His own no such infirm hand, Friday night;
> And next day, February Twenty Two,
> Since our salvation Sixteen Ninety Eight,
> —Not at the proper head-and-hanging place
> On bridge-foot close by Castle Angelo,
> Where custom somewhat staled the spectacle,
> ('Twas not so well i' the way of Rome, beside,
> The noble Rome, the Rome of Guido's rank)
> But at the city's newer gayer end,—
> The cavalcading promenading place
> Beside the gate and opposite the church
> Under the Pincian gardens green with spring,
> 'Neath the obelisk 'twixt the fountain in the Square,
> Did Guido and his fellows find their fate,
> All Rome for witness, and—my writer adds—
> Remonstrant in its universal grief,
> Since Guido had the suffrage of all Rome.
> This is the bookful; thus far take the truth,
> The untempered gold, the fact untampered with,
> The mere ring-metal ere the ring be made!
> And what has hitherto come of it? Who preserves
> The memory of this Guido and his wife
> Pompilia, more than Ademolla's name,
> The etcher of those prints, two *crazie* each,
> Saved by a stone from snowing broad the Square
> With scenic backgrounds? Was this truth of force?
> Able to take its own part as truth should,
> Sufficient, self-sustaining? Why, if so—
> Yonder's a fire, into it goes my book,
> As who shall say me nay, and what the loss?

129

There is a guiding unity in such writing as this, once one acquires the knack of finding it, but the writing is diverted from the subject as often as it remains with it, and by mere suggestion. I do not like Browning's method, although I am willing to admit that he uses the method with as much brilliance as the method admits, with an effect of baroque decoration which is very rich although tiresomely confusing; but I am not here concerned with the virtues or defects of Browning's method. I am concerned with the nature of the method, which is that of excited and consistent distraction. Robinson's method is that of hallucinated concentration, or at least of the mechanical imitation of hallucinated concentration as one finds such concentration in earlier New England writers. Browning buries his subject under irrelevancies, till it all but vanishes; Robinson subdivides his subject, and repeats and rearranges his subdivisions, till it all but vanishes. The result in each case is confusion; but the causative states of mind are widely different.

7. THE POEMS OF MEDIUM LENGTH

THE POEMS WHICH I HAVE IN MIND UNDER THIS HEADING ARE chiefly the following: From *Captain Craig, Etc.* (1902) "Isaac and Archibald," "Aunt Imogen" and "The Book of Annandale"; from *The Man Against the Sky* (1916) "Ben Jonson Entertains a Man from Stratford"; from *The Three Taverns* (1920) "The Three Taverns," "On the Way," "John Brown," "Tasker Norcross," "Rahel to Varnhagen" and "Lazarus"; from *Avon's Harvest, Etc.* (1921) "Rembrandt to Rembrandt"; from *Dionysus in Doubt* (1925) "Dionysus in Doubt," "Genevieve and Alexandra," "Mortmain," "Demos and Dionysus"; from *Nicodemus* (1932) "Nicodemus," "Sisera," "Toussaint L'Ouverture," "Ponce de Leon," "The March of the Cameron Men." I have somewhat arbitrarily chosen to discuss three of these poems, "On the Way," "Dionysus in Doubt" and "Demos and Dionysus" in the chapter on the shorter poems, for these poems deal with topics related to the topics of some of the shorter poems, and it seemed easiest to deal with them

131

there. I shall have to deal with the remaining poems some-what briefly, although a few of the best of Robinson's works are to be found in this group.

"Isaac and Archibald" is a kind of New England pastoral and is extraordinarily lovely. It deals with two old men, life-long friends, each of whom confided to the narrator, when he was a small boy, that the other was beginning to show signs of a weakening mind; for the rest, the poem describes the afternoon on which the confidences took place and the narrator's mature reflections on his memory of it. "Aunt Imogen" is what one might call a domestic poem of similar quality and similar excellence. It tells of the yearly visits of a maiden aunt to the home of her small nephews and niece and of the concentration of her mater-nal affection into this small experience. The poem could easily have been sentimental, but is not. It is not a great poem, but it is honest, perceptive and moving. We are told by Hagedorn [1] that "Isaac and Archibald" arose actu-ally from an experience that occurred in 1899 or 1900: "Al-fred Louis and William Henry Thorne had each confided in Robinson that he was convinced that the other was crazy, and both, Robinson wrote Mrs. Richards, had not been 'far wrong' "; and that "Aunt Imogen" [2] arose from his own feeling for his nieces. The first fact is amusing and the second touching, but I do not know that either adds much to our understanding of the poems and there is no certainty that either accounts for the poems except in a very small part. Hagedorn quotes William James [3] as saying that

[1] Op. cit., p. 168.
[2] Ibid., pp. 143–5.
[3] Ibid., p. 191.

"Isaac and Archibald" is "fully as good as anything of the kind in Wordsworth"; and the comment seems to me a fair one and might as fairly be made of "Aunt Imogen."

"The Book of Annandale" is very different. It offers, at this early date, a preliminary sketch of the method which Robinson was later to expand in the long narratives. It is divided into two sections. In the first, we learn that Annandale has just buried his young wife, with whom he had lived very happily for two or three years; he meditates upon his life with her, his loss, and a book which he had written and never shown her. In the second section, we are told of Damaris, who had remained faithful to the memory of her dead husband, Argan, for six or seven years. Gradually we discover that Annandale had wished to marry her after Argan's death and had written his book for her, and that when she refused he had married the wife whom he has since lost. At the end she realizes that she really loves Annandale and that a new life is beginning for her. The poem lacks the concentration of statement and the reality of setting of the first two poems which I have described, and it substitutes for the intensity which should arise from a perception of the situation a tension derived factitiously from the slow release of the necessary information. It is not, for example, till we are near the end of the second section that we receive any hint of the nature of the relationship between the two sections; this is not art, but rather is a technique of systematic exasperation.

"Ben Jonson Entertains a Man from Stratford" is definitely a Browningesque monologue. It is composed entirely of what Jonson said to his guest. The poem is in part a portrait of Jonson, who does the talking, and in part a portrait of Shakespeare, of whom Jonson talks. The poem has been more widely praised than most of Robinson's poems, but it seems to me no more than a secondary poem at best. In the manner of Browning, Robinson endeavors to display the character of his speaker by displaying the mannerisms of his speech; and again in the manner of Browning he succeeds merely in displaying the unchecked mannerisms of the poet. If one compares Robinson's Jonson to the Jonson of the plays, poems, and Drummond fragments, Robinson's Jonson appears frail, nervous, and shallow—he bears about the same relationship to the original that Robinson's Tristram bears to the Tristram of the Old French poet, Thomas. The portrait of Shakespeare, the ostensible subject of the poem, is diffused among the mannerisms, and even when one puts it all together one has perhaps less than one can find in history, and that is very little indeed. The blank verse is in some ways an improvement on that of the earlier poems; it is quicker and more limber; but the substance of the poem is slight.

"The Three Taverns" is an address by Paul the Apostle to the Christians who came out to meet him as he approached Rome toward the end of his career. It is partly a summary of his career and mainly an explanation of it. Robinson is dealing in this poem with a single-minded man of great intensity and dignity, whose purpose so far transcends all other aspects of his character as to render them negligible. Paul is a man whose doctrines and character have always been especially sympathetic to the Protestant mind: he is the first great voluntarist and fideist, the man who set faith and will above understanding, the man who was struck down on the highway by the sudden vision of

God and whose conversion was a kind of model of the violent and more or less mystical conversions so common among the Calvinists. But the treatment of Paul in Robinson's poem is restrained and cautious: Paul is the man who will not recognize that the Law is sacrosanct merely because it is established; who insists that there may be closer approximations to truth than those already made; who insists upon the value of the percept as well as of the concept; who is troubled by the hazards of personal judgment yet remains convinced that his judgment of his own experience is true. The drama of the poem, if one may call it drama, resides in the struggle between the conviction of rightness and the awareness of the hazards: the poem deals with the ultimate decision possible to man, with the sacrifice of life for the salvation of the soul.

> See "The Three Taverns," lines
> 29-35 on page 470 and lines 1-2 on
> page 471 of *Collected Poems* of
> Robinson.

This theme, in the barest possible terms, is identical with the theme of *Lancelot*, and with certain minor modifications resembles the theme of "John Brown" and of "Rembrandt to Rembrandt." John Brown is less troubled than Paul with a sense of the complexity of things, is more direct in his statement of his assurance, but otherwise the resemblance between the poems is strong. In "Rembrandt to Rembrandt" the theme is modified to this extent: the artist is faced with the question of the rightness of his belief in his own ability and in what he is doing as an artist; and by this modification the theme is brought very close to the central obsession of Robinson's personal experience.

In "The Three Taverns," there is no conflict between characters and no occasion for characters to argue, dissect and conceal, as there is in the longer poems; we have a great mind, of whom the records are remarkably full, drawing itself together to meet its end. Robinson handles the material as it should be handled; he does not expand it, but he contracts it to essentials; he exhibits the greatness of the man, not the mannerisms of his speech. The poem is bare of all decoration, and is written in a blank verse which is compact and well organized. It is one of the greatest poems of its kind and length in English. The opening paragraph is typical of the style.

> See "The Three Taverns," lines 1-
> 9 on page 461 and lines 1-30 on
> page 463 of *Collected Poems* of
> Robinson.

The language offers no superficial enticements, and if read carelessly may seem to have little life; but as one understands it more precisely it gathers force.

"John Brown" is a shorter poem than "The Three Taverns," and deals with a character of more restricted intelligence and importance, though an impressive one. The poem consists of a speech by John Brown to his wife the night before his death, in which he justifies himself, expresses pity for his wife and faces his end. I have the feeling that the poem is not quite so uniformly distinguished in its language as the poem on Paul, but the feeling would be hard to demonstrate, for the language is nowhere really bad. One of the finest passages in the poem is John Brown's adjuration to his wife.

See "John Brown," lines 27-34 on page 488 and lines 1-9 on page 489 of *Collected Poems* of Robinson.

"Tasker Norcross" is a less interesting poem and exhibits two of Robinson's mannerisms, though less obviously than do some of the long poems—his loquacity and his habit of withholding information in order to lead one to a surprise ending—but it is a good sketch of a lonely and unhappy New England character. "Rahel to Varnhagen" is a curious poem in its quiet way of moving one, but it is both minor and imperfect. Robinson precedes it with a note: "Rahel Robert and Varnhagen von Ense were married, after many protestations on her part, in 1814. The marriage—so far as he was concerned at any rate—appears to have been satisfactory." The poem is a speech by the elderly lady to her young lover, which terminates in her acquiescence. The poem is direct and not too long, and on the whole is excellent, but is marred by moments of Robinson's inept playfulness.

See "Rahel to Varnhagen," lines 11-18 on page 515 [4], lines 3-6 on

[4] This entire passage is feeble enough, but it is the last line, of course, which makes one really wince. One might note also the use of *diamonds* first as trisyllabic and in the next line as dissyllabic. Robinson's meter is not often quite so careless.

> page 516 and lines 14-21 on page
> 520 of *Collected Poems* of Robin-
> son.

The entire conclusion is very weak, but the colloquial phrase, *so dismal much,* and the last line, are especially unfortunate.

"Lazarus" consists largely of a conversation between Martha and Mary and of a second conversation between Mary and Lazarus, after the return of Lazarus from the dead. The theme of the poem is the unbridgeable separation between life and death and the insoluble mystery of both. My description is vague of necessity, but the poem has great power and the style is controlled in every line.

> See "Lazarus," lines 3-11 on page
> 539 of *Collected Poems* of Robin-
> son.

"Lazarus" is less great than "The Three Taverns" chiefly, I think, by virtue of the fact that the subject of "The Three Taverns" can be treated directly, whereas the subject of "Lazarus" can be treated only by indirection, suggestion and withdrawal; "Lazarus" is an attempt to indicate the limits of the inexpressible.

"Rembrandt to Rembrandt" is in the form of a soliloquy by the painter, or rather of an address, presumably a silent one, which he makes in the decline of his popularity to a portrait which he had painted of himself earlier in his career. It is a study in the bitterness of the neglected artist and in his doubts of himself, a subject which Robinson felt as a personal one. It is not the easiest of reading, but such difficulty as it offers is not factitious; it is the result of profound perception and extremely close and careful language. As in "The Three Taverns" and the great rimed poem of about the same period, "The Wandering Jew," the language is largely abstract, and its power resides in the great concentration and generality of reference which can be achieved with such language; the great poems of *The Man Against the Sky* are open and obvious, both in plan and in perception, as compared to these three poems. Two passages will illustrate the style.

> See "Rembrandt to Rembrandt,"
> lines 8-17 on page 590 and lines
> 25-34 on page 591 [5] of *Collected*
> *Poems* of Robinson.

If I were to single out one of Robinson's poems in blank verse as perhaps the greatest, with respect both to scope of subject and to mastery of language, this, I believe, would be the poem, in spite of my great admiration for a few others; it stands in this respect with "The Wandering Jew" among the poems in rimed stanzas, and with "Many Are Called" among the sonnets.

"Genevieve and Alexandra" is a dramatic dialogue between two women about a man; it is trivial in conception and in execution. "Mortmain" deals with a frustrated romance between two elderly New Englanders; in general intention it is similar to "Isaac and Archibald" and to "Aunt

[5] The widowed gold, in line 32, I take it, was the estate inherited from his wife, Saskia.

Imogen," but approaches much less nearly to perfection, chiefly because of a moderate admixture of the pedantic playfulness of style to which Robinson is often given. "Nicodemus" is composed largely of a dialogue between Nicodemus, a young Jewish gentleman who has recently become a follower of Jesus, and Caiaphas, a priest and his friend, who regards the whole business as foolishness. The poem is excellent in its plan and is for the most part respectable in style, though a brief emotional outburst from Nicodemus near the end is very weak. The style, however, is relaxed and a trifle flat as compared to the style of the greater poems, and the piece is hardly one of the important works. "Sisera" tells the familiar Biblical story of Sisera and Jael; the narrative is plain and direct, but the style is undistinguished. "Toussaint L'Ouverture" and "Ponce de Leon" are both monologues by the protagonists just before death. The subjects are good, and the general idea of each poem is at least fairly good, but the poems give the impression of having been written in haste to an old formula; the first is an expression of emotion, primarily, with insufficient generalization of its meaning, and toward the end especially it tends to break down into weak ejaculation; the second is about as nearly effective as "Nicodemus." "The March of the Cameron Men" is a dialogue between a man and a woman. The man is a physician and has just permitted the woman's husband to die so that the two will be free to love each other. The woman is moved by remorse and decides that the two of them must see no more of each other. The conversation is too long and too subtle for the occasion and the writing is nowhere remarkable. The poem takes its name from a song, of which we are given certain stanzas, and which is in some fashion symbolic of the woman's remorse, although the symbolism remains extremely vague and is wholly unnecessary to the poem.

In review of these poems one may say that there are two which rank among the greatest of their kind in English, "Rembrandt to Rembrandt" and "The Three Taverns," and that two others, "Lazarus" and "John Brown," are great poems; that two, "Isaac and Archibald" and "Aunt Imogen," are among the most successful of Robinson's minor poems; and that among the rest there are at least a few which are memorable. The volumes containing the best of these poems appeared in the years 1920 and 1921 and contain three of the greatest of the shorter poems, "The Wandering Jew," "Lost Anchors" and "Many Are Called," as well as seven or eight other short pieces of very high quality. *Lancelot* appeared in 1920. The works of these years represent, I think, an even higher achievement than that reached in *The Man Against the Sky*, a book which is frequently mentioned as the high point in Robinson's career. *Dionysus in Doubt* (1925) contains one great poem, "The Sheaves" (a sonnet previously mentioned), and a few short pieces which are excellent; but from here onward the quality of Robinson's work declines seriously and rapidly, and there is little to praise except a few passages in *Amaranth,* and those in moderation. The period of depression is that of the last ten years. What the cause of it may have been one can only guess: it may have been a diminution of his powers, preliminary to his final illness; it may have been hasty writing, resulting from his discovery that his poems could earn him an income and from his old discomfort at being dependent upon others for his support; it may have been an honest but misguided interest in a kind of poem of which he had too little understanding; but as I have already said, he devoted himself mainly in this period to long poems, for which even in the years of his greatest achievement he had shown a marked incapacity, and he wrote too much and apparently published about all that he wrote.

8. CONCLUSION

I HAVE EXPRESSED MY BELIEF THAT ROBINSON'S LONG POEMS are mostly unsuccessful and represent a waste of effort; that the best of them is *Lancelot*, an impressive poem in spite of many imperfections, and that *Merlin*, though it is hardly a great poem, contains great poetry; that Robinson's most successful work is to be found among his shorter poems and poems of medium length, of which we may cite for the moment such examples as "Hillcrest," "Eros Turannos," "The Wandering Jew," "Many Are Called," "The Three Taverns" and "Rembrandt to Rembrandt." Of Robinson's more obvious faults I have already said enough. There remain certain questions of more or less interest: What kind of relationship does Robinson have to the poets who precede and who follow him? To what extent do any of his weaknesses affect his great poetry? How does he compare to the other great poets, American or British, who have written in English?

In the second decade of the present century, when the

143

so-called poetic Renaissance was at the height of its reputation and when Robinson was beginning to attract attention, it was common to see Robinson mentioned as a forerunner of such poets as Masters, Lindsay and Sandburg, and there is still a tendency to refer to him as a kind of ancestor of much or all of that which has come since. The origin of this idea is apparently to be found in the directness and honesty of his style, as if, in the first place, such a quality were new, and as if, in the second place, it were characteristic of the poetry in question. Nothing, I think, could be less judicious. Masters, Lindsay and Sandburg are sentimental poets with no gift for thought and no command of their craft; the first two are forgotten except as they survive in high school curricula, and the third will soon follow them; they belong to a generation which mistook the inept outburst of the amateur for the direct statement of honesty. The more talented poets of the same period, such as Pound and Eliot, represent a conscious effort to dissolve thought and structure in feeling and in sensory perception, and the poetry which has proceeded from them, the bulk of the poetry of the past two decades, exhibits the same tendency in talents which are, for the most part, less impressive than the talents of Lindsay and Sandburg. Stevens is similar to Pound and Eliot in this respect, except for a few of his earlier poems, such as "Sunday Morning"; but Stevens in his thought is committed to the process of dissolution which in the main he follows, and his best poetry resembles Robinson only in its exhibition of a great native gift and a traditional method. Louise Bogan writes in a style as purely classical as that of Robinson, but her sources, so far as they appear, are in the sixteenth and seventeenth centuries; and although she is one of the best poets of our time, she is hardly characteristic of our time or at least of what passes for it among our poets and critics. Frost resembles Robinson more closely than does any other, but the resemblance is stronger upon first glance than upon second and tends to disappear with re-examination. The resemblance is strongest between such poems as "Isaac and Archibald" and some of Frost's narratives in blank verse; but the resemblance depends mainly upon the brute and impersonal fact that both poets come from much the same part of the country and sometimes write about it. The resemblance is in part due to the fact that Robinson is more nearly colloquial in a few such minor poems as this than he is in his greater and that Frost has tended to make a discreet mannerism of colloquial speech (which is not quite the same thing as the plain speech of the man of letters, such as one finds in Robinson's greatest work). The resemblance is due in part also to the fact that this poem by Robinson is minor: Frost is an Emersonian Romantic who celebrates the minor incident, the eccentric attitude and the fleeting perception; he frequently does it with extraordinary beauty, and I trust will long remain an ornament to our literature, but to compare him to the author of "The Wandering Jew" and of "Rembrandt to Rembrandt," on the grounds either of resemblance or of greatness, is pointless.

I have already mentioned the poets who seem to me to have influenced Robinson; the two most considerable influences, I believe, are Browning and Praed. But of these, Browning is an influence only on a small portion of Robinson's work, and not on a very important portion, and Praed at most is merely a point of departure. If one tries to compare Robinson to practitioners of the other forms of literature, one runs the risk of being superficial and perhaps inaccurate, but the effort, if not taken too seriously, may have a little value; and it has long appeared to me that his closest spiritual relatives, at least in America, are to be found in the writers of fiction and of history in his generation and the two or three generations preceding. I have called attention to his having certain more or less Jamesian vices as a narrator, but I am thinking now of his virtues: of the plain style, the rational statement, the psychological insight, the subdued irony, the high seriousness and the stubborn persistence. In respect to one or another of these qualities, one may find him related to such a mind as that of Henry James, but perhaps more obviously to Edith Wharton and Motley and Francis Parkman, and perhaps even at times to Henry Adams. He is, it seems to me, the last great American writer of their tradition and not the first of a later one; and the fact that he writes verse is incidental. There was little verse of major importance produced in this country in the nineteenth century and in the early twentieth; there was a good deal of major prose; and Robinson is more closely comparable to the great masters of prose than to the minor poets.

In reading Robinson's verse during a period of approximately twenty-five years, I have always felt a certain deficiency, even in some of the best of it, and I have heard the same deficiency mentioned by other readers: the deficiency is easy to indicate—it is a certain dryness, a lack of richness in the language—but it is not so easy to define with any precision. One may read such a poem as "Hillcrest," admire it and recognize its greatness, and yet feel, however fallaciously, that one has more or less exhausted its interest after a few readings; whereas one is likely to return repeatedly to such poems as George Herbert's "Church Monuments" or Robert Bridges' "Dejection." It is hard to lay one's finger on the precise reason. I have chosen these two poems by Herbert and Bridges because they forestall what might seem the most obvious explanation: the intellectuality of Robinson and his relative freedom from sensory imagery. These poems are at least equally intellectual and are quite as free from sensory imagery, and one could easily add other poems to the list: "Down in the depths of mine iniquity," by Greville; "If Beauty be the mark of praise," by Jonson; and "Thou hast made me," by Donne; and these are only a few. I think the explanation may lie in two causes, which are perhaps related, and which I have already discussed: a certain deficiency in Robinson's ear, which results at times in a somewhat mechanical and imperceptive rhythm—I am referring not to his meters or his stanzas, but to the way he uses them—and a distrust of the suggestive power of language in favor of an unnecessary fullness of expository statement, a fullness which sometimes degenerates into simple cleverness. In regard to the second point, I am not objecting either to the rational structure of his poems or to their rational content, for of those the reader must by now be aware that I approve; but to a slightly unnecessary subdivision and restatement of matter, a slight lack of concentration. These defects are the defects of Praed and Holmes and poets of their type, of poets who may be skillful, ingenious, civilized and amusing, but who are not quite serious about their subjects and

147

not quite masters of their language. In Robinson's weaker poems, especially in his narratives, the defects are deadly. In his secondary successes, such as "Two Gardens in Linndale," they are very obvious; and one feels them in some of his greater poems, slightly in "Hillcrest" and "Eros Turannos" and plainly in "For a Dead Lady." On the other hand these defects are diminished to the point of being negligible in such poems as "Veteran Sirens," "The Wandering Jew," "Many Are Called," "The Three Taverns" and "Rembrandt to Rembrandt." If the tide ever sets against Robinson's reputation—and if it does not, sooner or later, his reputation will be an exceptional one—I think that these defects will be the reason. But it seems to me that the defects are merely defects, like any others, and should be given no more importance than the defects of many another great poet. The vatic pomposity of Wordsworth is ruinous to most of his work and can be detected in his best; the grammatical machinery of Milton's sonnets is almost always a little too great for the occasion and sometimes endeavors to enforce unity upon unrelated matter; and there is the excessive ingenuity of the Metaphysical School. It is unfortunate that Robinson published so voluminously, for one becomes irritated in reading him through, just as one becomes irritated in reading Wordsworth or Tennyson, and one becomes nervously aware of his faults and is inclined to see them even where they do not appear. No poet can publish in this manner with impunity, and as time goes by the risk will become progressively greater: even a genius as great as Wordsworth, a hundred or two hundred years hence, might succeed in burying his worth under the mountains of his mediocrity.

148

CONCLUSION

These defects are the initial defects of a manner and a temperament, defects which Robinson held under reasonable control in a great many poems, and eliminated, or all but eliminated, from seven or eight. In the diminution of these faults and in the more or less comparable process of universalizing his New England mind, he became on certain occasions one of the most remarkable poets in our language. His style at its best is as free from the provincialism of time and of place as the best writing of Jonson or Herbert. This impersonal greatness of style has been seldom achieved in the twentieth century; one finds it in some of the greatest work of the nineteenth century poets: in the "Ode to Duty," by Wordsworth; in "Tiresias," by Tennyson; in parts of "The Pope," from *The Ring and the Book;* in a number of lyrics by Hardy, such as "In the Time of the Breaking of Nations"; and above all, perhaps, in a few poems by Bridges: for example, in "Dejection," "Eros," "Low Barometer" and "The Affliction of Richard." It is among these British poets of the last century and of the turn of the century that Robinson seems at moments to find his closest relatives and quite possibly his closest rivals on this side of Milton and Dryden; and his position in relation to these poets is not that of the lowest.

BIBLIOGRAPHY

The amount of material published on Robinson is very great, and it has been well listed in the bibliographies which I have named at the end of these few titles. I have endeavored merely to provide a list of Robinson's important publications, with their dates, for the reader's convenience, and to provide a brief introduction to the general criticism of Robinson in case the reader is interested. Only a little of this material, I may as well confess, has been of any great value to myself, and if I were to limit my bibliography to the titles of works that seem to me genuinely helpful, it would be very brief indeed. I especially recommend Mr. Hogan's bibliography, partly because of its value as a list of titles, partly because it reprints a number of items not easily found elsewhere. Of the criticism I should recommend the items by Hoyt H. Hudson, Louise Bogan and W. T. Scott, and with reservations those by M. D. Zabel and Allen Tate. For the rest, I have tried to give specimens of opinion on Robinson by a few of our more distinguished critics and by certain professional scholars who have devoted more or less time to him. I have tried to offer various opinions and schools of criticism. I am in complete disagreement with some of the writers listed; in fact, a few of the items, so far as I am concerned, may be taken merely as horrible examples of what the critic should never do.

BIBLIOGRAPHY

I. EDWIN ARLINGTON ROBINSON

1. Poems

The Torrent and the Night Before, Cambridge, Mass., 1896.
The Children of the Night, Boston, 1897.
Captain Craig, Boston and New York, 1902.
The Town Down the River, New York, 1910.
The Man Against the Sky, New York, 1916.
Merlin, New York, 1917.
Lancelot, New York, 1920.
The Three Taverns, New York, 1920.
Avon's Harvest, New York, 1921.
Collected Poems, New York, 1921.
Roman Bartholow, New York, 1923.
The Man Who Died Twice, New York, 1924.
Dionysus in Doubt, New York, 1925.
Tristram, New York, 1927.
Sonnets 1889–1927, New York, 1928.
Cavender's House, New York, 1929.
Collected Poems, New York, 1929.
The Glory of the Nightingales, New York, 1930.
Selected Poems, with a Preface by Bliss Perry, New York, 1931.
Matthias at the Door, New York, 1932.
Nicodemus, New York, 1932.
Talifer, New York, 1933.
Amaranth, New York, 1934.
King Jasper, New York, 1935.
Collected Poems, New York, 1937.

2. Letters

Selected Letters of Edwin Arlington Robinson. Introduction by Ridgely Torrence, New York, 1940.

3. Biography

Edwin Arlington Robinson, a Biography, by Herman Hagedorn, New York, 1938.

151

II. SECONDARY STUDIES (Select List)

1. Books

Cestre, Charles, *An Introduction to Edwin Arlington Robinson*, 1930.

Kaplan, Estelle, *Philosophy in the Poetry of Edwin Arlington Robinson*, 1940.

Morris, Lloyd, *The Poetry of Edwin Arlington Robinson*, 1923.

Redman, Ben Ray, *Edwin Arlington Robinson*, 1928.

Van Doren, Mark, *Edwin Arlington Robinson*, 1927.

2. Articles

Blackmur, R. P., "Verse that is too easie," *Poetry*, January, 1934.

Bogan, Louise, "Tilbury Town and Beyond," *Poetry*, January, 1931.

Carpenter, F. I., "Tristram the Transcendent," *New England Quarterly*, September, 1938.

Colum, Mary M., "Poets and Their Problems," *The Forum*, June, 1935.

Dauner, L., "Vox clamantis: E. A. R. as a Critic of American Democracy," *New England Quarterly*, September, 1942.

Evans, Nancy, "Edwin Arlington Robinson," *The Bookman*, November, 1932.

Gorman, Herbert S., "Edwin Arlington Robinson," *The New Republic*, February, 1922.

Hudson, Hoyt H., "Robinson and Praed," *Poetry*, February, 1943.

Mather, F. J., Jr., "E. A. Robinson: poet," *Saturday Review of Literature*, January, 1930.

Monroe, Harriet, "Edwin Arlington Robinson," *Poetry*, January, 1925.

——, "Robinson as Man and Poet," *Poetry*, June, 1935.

Ransom, John Crowe, "Autumn of Poetry," *Southern Review*, Winter, 1936.

Roosevelt, Theodore, "The Children of the Night," *The Outlook*, August, 1905.

Scott, Winfield T., "Unaccredited Profession," *Poetry*, June, 1937.

——, "Robinson to Robinson," *Poetry*, May, 1939.

BIBLIOGRAPHY

Stovall, Floyd, "The Optimism behind Robinson Tragedies," *American Literature*, March, 1938.

Tate, Allen, "Again, O Ye Laurels," *The New Republic*, October, 1933.

Zabel, M. D., "Robinson in America," *Poetry*, 1935.

——, "Robinson: the Ironic Discipline," *The Nation*, August, 1937.

3. Bibliographies

Beebe, Lucius M., and Bulkley, Robert J., *Bibliography of the Writings of Edwin Arlington Robinson*, 1931.

Hogan, Charles B., *A Bibliography of Edwin Arlington Robinson*, 1936.

Lippincott, Lillian, *A Bibliography of the Writings and Criticisms of Edwin Arlington Robinson*, 1937.

Millett, Fred B., *Contemporary American Authors*, 1940, pp. 549–554.

INDEX

INDEX

INDEX

INDEX